The Unlikely Celebrity

The Unlikely Celebrity

Bill Sackter's Triumph over Disability

Thomas Walz

With a Foreword by Barry Morrow

Southern Illinois University Press
Carbondale and Edwardsville

01 00 99 98   4 3 2 1

Library of Congress Cataloging-in-Publication Data
Walz, Thomas, 1933–
    The unlikely celebrity : Bill Sackter's triumph over disability /
Thomas Walz ; with a foreword by Barry Morrow.
        p.   cm.

    1. Sackter, Bill. 2. Mentally handicapped—Iowa—Biography.
3. Coffee shops—Iowa—Employees—Biography. I. Title.
HV3006.S33W35 1998
362.3'092—dc21   98-6260
[B]   CIP
ISBN 0-8093-2134-3 (cloth : alk. paper)
ISBN 0-8093-2213-7 (pbk : alk. paper)

The paper used in this publication meets the minimum requirements of American National Standard for Information Sciences—Permanence of Paper for
Printed Library Materials, ANSI Z39.48-1984.   ∞

Contents

Illustrations

Foreword

In the misty mid-sixties, my best school chum and I, answering the call of Kerouac and Dylan, would often haunt the lower streets of downtown Minneapolis looking to get lost. Slouched in the doorways of coffee shops or three-dollar hotels, wearing our Goodwill rags, we tried to act tough, talk tough, be weird, be cool, like Destitute Drifters. Yeah. One night in March 1968, we hopped a freight train for Breckenridge, Colorado, riding it a hundred yards before jumping off again. Boys from the suburbs, too cool to be cold.

A half-dozen years later, I met the real deal—a man with no agenda, no money, no family, no teeth, no future, and no direction home. He said his name was Bill, William, and he didn't know Dylan or Kerouac. But he could change lives.

For a dozen years, he was the Destitute Drifter who stayed. He found the soft core in all who stumbled across his path, beguiling us with his innocence, conning us with his grin, sapping us of our patience, but mostly, and most importantly, transfusing us with his goodness. A man of many limitations, Bill was slow to reveal his more plentiful gifts, but in time, we came to see him for what he was: a friend and counselor, a shaper of lives, and the catalyst of at least one career. I didn't plan to be a screenwriter. I just met Bill Sackter. I have often been credited, largely by myself, as the key force in shaping Bill's life. That's what happens when it's your typewriter. But if history has any say in this, there would have to be some small mention of Old Tom.

Old Tom, the author of this book, was Bill's friend. He has been an educator, lecturer, social activist, and woodworker. He is still all those things (except old; Bill just called him that out of deep respect). From the beginning, Tom was not only drawn to Bill, he was drawn to the *idea* of Bill. "What man was this? And why?" While these questions had struck others, they gripped Tom. Bill Sackter was the riddle within a riddle: Despite a lifetime of deprivation, he gave freely of all he had; despite his severe limitations, he had faith that all was possible; despite the cruelties aimed at him, he stayed kind. Yet Bill was more than the perfect metaphor. He was real.

In *The Unlikely Celebrity*, Tom Walz comes closer than anyone yet in explaining the genesis of Bill's legend, the resonance of his life, and the mythic hold it continues to have on our hearts.

With warmth, wit, and engaging style—with respect for all the players in this saga—Tom takes us to a place where the air is clear. There, looking back, we see now that in our search to know Bill, we were really looking for ourselves. His struggle was our struggle: that we might be good, too. What a happy, boundless idea.

—Barry Morrow

Preface

The name is William Sackter, though most of my life I would tell peoples to call me Bill. Once in a while, a few frens would call me "Wild Bill from Borneo" or jus plain buddy. I think they would call me buddy cause I always called them buddy, and I always called 'em buddy cause I could never member their darn names. When I do member names, I get 'em wrong. Like my good buddy, Barry Morrow, the bes I could member was "Barrymor." Mostly, he was jus buddy. Tom, he was Tom (never could member his last name), and Tom's dog, he was Roloff. Tom tol me I confused Roloff with a television preacher I use-ta send money to. To be trufful, for a long time, I did'n even know who William was. It was'n till I was a grown man that I figured out Bill was short for William.

As you will soon find out, if you have'n already guessed, God did'n pass out so many brains in my directions. I never learned to read 'n write. I never even learned to dial a phone, ride a bike, or drives a car. Once't I did drive a tractor and scared the life out of Barry's neighbor, Chiles. You'll hear bout that story later from ol Tom.

Not bein' so smart of mind, I used to think of myself as a "crack-minded man." I s'pose all those years in the isstitution peoples would make fun of me and call me a crack-minded man, and it started me thinkin' of myself in that way. I might-a been dumb. I know I was too dumb for regular school. That's why they sent me to a state school. But I still could manage my own things my mind could'n handle. Not being the smartest guy downtown, I learned the bes thing was to have lots of buddies. Jus like in gettin' this story written, I am askin' my ol buddy Tom to writes it.

Now in truf, I never did figure out what all the fuss was bout when I was in Iowa. For most of my life, I hardly talks to peoples, and peoples hardly talks to me. On a good day, folks lef me alone, and I lef 'em alone. I learned if you 'voided the aides in the isstitution, you could 'void troubles for yourself. Then one day, I was in the middle of peoples havin' fun when I was round. Like with Barrymor and his frens. Peoples seemed to like my playin' the mouf organ, and they were always laughin' when I was round. Maybe they jus liked the ways I played. I know Mae Driscoll, my landlady, and the peoples that lived there, like Kenny and Angela, they were always askin' me to play.

Tom thinks if I tell my storys, it'll be good for other crack-minded peoples. They can see that even though I was'n smart, I did have me a good life in the end.

Anyways, I 'greed to do most-a the speakin', if ol Tom'll jus do the writin'. He says ol Jim'll help somes, too. So if anybuddy goin' tell any stories, it'll be ol Bill hisself. Do you know some folks in Hollywood once't made a movie bout my life using my name—Bill. I saw it on TV. Tom said it was s'posed to be bout my life, but when I saw it, it was bout Mickey Roomie's life. Peoples once asked me if I thought Mickey Roomies played my lifes good. I could only tell 'em that I thought ol Mickey was quite a fellow and that he had himself a life a lot like mine. He had some hard times, you know. He was fond-a childern. I liked him for that, cause I likes playin' with childern. Ol Roomies, he liked eatin' chicken, too, jus like me. But he eats too much, and this young guy gets mad at him. Barry used to get mad at me when I starts gobblin' down chicken at his place. I love chicken.

Tellin' my story isn't goin' to be easy. I got the memory of a rock. My chilehood fore I get put in the isstitution don't member much to me. I got some powerful feelin's and few pitchures in my mind, but the rest is pretty muddy. There's jus a few things I can member, and ol Tom will tell you bout these later, like some problems I had wettin' my pants at school. I could'n get the right words out to tells the teacher I had to go to the toilets. Schools always got my mind muzzled. If my mother or my sister had'n taken me right to the door of the classroom, I think I'd still be loss. Anyways, what I can't member, Tom and Jim Dooley can tell you. They spent a lot of time tryin' to find out bout me. I don't really care much bout the ol times. They were bad, buddy. It's the good times that I cares bout.

There are only a few things bout my chilehood and my lifes in the isstitution I can member. But I member lots more bout Iowa Citys with my buddies and frens. Maybe it's not jus being dumb that makes me not member, but jus that I don't like thinkin' bout bad stuff that happened. I had too many hard times, buddy, and I'm jus happy now I got the good times. Iowa was the good times for me. I had lots of frens—Barrymor, the Rabbi Portman, John Crass, Fat John, Mae, Kenny and Angela, and you, too, Tom. They were nice to me, and I try to give 'em some happiness. When I could make peoples happy, it made me happy.

Tom seemed to think I was really somebuddy special, like one of God's chosen or somethin'. If he wants to think that way, ain't nothin' I can do. But so's you know, I was really jus a crack-minded person who found me a different world by lookin' to its happy side instead of its bad side. I learned that what you see is what you is, and I was tired of bad things happenin' to me. All I wants is the good things now—lotsa frens, a good sandwiches in my lunch box, some polka music, and maybe even a big cigar from ol John. Also, I'd like a beer now and then.

So jus go ahead and tell my story, especially if it helps other crack-minded peoples. Barrymor got me set free in my life, and Tom gave me a job. That's bout all anybuddy can ask.

Shalom, God loves you.

Bill's story, or at least a part of it, has been told before but not in print. In 1981, a television movie entitled *Bill* told of some of his experiences after he had left the institution for the retarded and epileptic in which he had been confined for forty-four years. The movie proved so popular that it led to a rare sequel called *Bill on His Own*, which was aired in December 1983. The second film intended to give an even more favorable and more accurate portrayal of Bill and something more of the story that documented the basis of his popularity.

Bill was born in Minneapolis, Minnesota, in 1913, the son of Russian Jewish immigrant parents, Sam Sackter and Mary Masnick. He would enter Faribault State School in 1920, then known as the State School for Feeble-Minded and Epileptics, as a seven-year-old child. Bill would remain there for the next four-and-a-half decades. His admission was occasioned by his intellectual limitations, problems with bladder control, and the difficulties his mother had in caring for three children after the sudden death of Bill's father in 1920.

However, the coming of deinstitutionalization in the mental health movement would thrust Bill back onto the streets of Minneapolis in the mid-1960s. For the next ten years, he would drift aimlessly, living in a series of board-and-room homes as a ward of the state until a serendipitous event took place: Bill would come to the attention of a young couple, Bev and Barry Morrow. Within a short time, Barry would petition for the guardianship of Bill and be awarded custody. Not long afterward, Barry would take a job at the University of Iowa and would bring Bill along. Both would end up employed in the University of Iowa's School of Social Work where I served as the director.

Bill would be given a variety of jobs in the school, but his fame would be built upon his job as sole proprietor of Wild Bill's Coffeeshop, which served the students, staff, and faculty who officed or studied in North Hall on the University of Iowa campus. Bill's antics and exploits here gave birth to hundreds of stories that would later be told about him.

Bill would go on to become a minor national celebrity as a result of the television movies about his life. His onetime guardian, Barry Morrow, would attain an even more lofty celebrity status as the Emmy Award-winning cowriter of the story for the movie *Bill*, and later, as the Oscar-winning screenwriter of the film *Rain Man*. Barry is now a Hollywood movie producer, with plans to direct more feature films.

This book is Bill's story as Bill might have told it, had God given him the memory and the vocabulary to do so. Thus, some of the facts and some of the interpretations of events require the voice of another commentator. That voice is mine. Bill was very much a companion during his eight short, but illustrious years as proprietor of Wild Bill's Coffeeshop in the School of Social Work.

The reason for its telling? Bill was truly a special human being. He was a gentle man whose innocence, caring, and kindness made him into a sort of Pied Piper for both children and adults. His following was quite unlike anything there had ever been in the laid-back college town of Iowa City, the place where he lived out those final eight years of his life.

When Bill died on June 16, 1983, flags were flown at half-mast by both the city and the university. In my twenty-five years in this community, this is the only time I am aware of this happening. It is not often that a man of Bill's intellect and background has commanded such public regard. This is both a testimony to him and a reminder to us not to overlook some truly remarkable people in our communities who may, at first blush, appear to be different.

It is my own belief that Bill has earned a right to a small niche in American mythology. You be the judge.

Acknowledgments

Like a twice-baked potato, this is a twice-written book. A more or less straight biographical effort was made the first time through to tell Bill's story. As it stood upon its completion, I felt it an injustice to Bill and what I hoped he would represent to the reader. So for five years, I let the manuscript rest on a shelf and gather dust. Finally, with the help of a sabbatical, I made a commitment for better or worse to complete the project. Bill's real story, I felt, had not yet been told, despite the two television movies in his name.

Whatever its shortcomings, I think this current effort comes much closer to being Bill's story since he narrates a good share of it. His voice approximates much more his understanding and feelings about his life. The first acknowledgment, therefore, must go to Bill Sackter, the man of the story, whose life and voice is what the reader experiences. The energy in the story, however, must be credited to Bill's friend and guardian, Barry Morrow. Barry provided the stage where Bill honed his craft. Barry gave Bill a doorway to self-confidence. Once Bill passed through this doorway, he was clearly "on his own" (the title of the sequel movie comes from this idea), and the rest belongs largely to him and his retinue of friends.

The silent partner in the research and writing of this manuscript is Jim Dooley, an Iowa City native and former public affairs director of a major television station. Over a two-year period, with little or no resources to support him, Jim painstakingly explored Bill's later years as an inmate in Faribault State School. Much of the actual language used in those chapters belongs to Jim.

Thanks must also be shared with the secretarial staff of the School of Social Work at the University of Iowa, particularly Bev Sweet, who diligently typed the early manuscripts, and Mika Uematsu, a young writer and editor who professionally edited the final version of the manuscript before its departure to the publisher.

In all, writing Bill's book, like the cliché suggests, has been a labor of love. It completes a project that I felt was essential to finish as my professional life draws to a close. Because I have both a brother and a son who are mentally challenged, I wanted to put this story into the hands of those who have struggled to normalize life for their mentally challenged loved ones. I also dreamed that others, less aware of the pervasiveness of mental retardation in society, would find that the book clarifies many misconceptions they may have had about this developmental disability.

1

Growing Up Scared

I wished I could member more bout my growin' up. I do member some bout my mother, jus a little bout my papa, and mos bout my sister—Sara. I think Sara was the one takin' care-a me when my folks was runnin' the grocery store in north Minneapolis.

To the bes of my memories, we had our livin' quarters above the store. Seems like I was livin' above somethin' or other most of my life. When I was washin' pots 'n pans at the Middykata (Minikahda) Club, my sleeping room was above the kitchen. Jim Dooley says my folks' store was somewheres in north Minneapolis where all the Jewish peoples lived. My grandma had a store on the same block as my folks, though I don't member nothin' bout her. My mama was her little girl.

My papa's folks lived in the Ol Country—somewheres in Russia. Jim says they were from the Ukraine and wanted to go to America cause the 'ficials were gettin' awful mean to Jewish peoples. They would start riots 'n try to get rid of Jewish peoples or punish 'em for being Jewish.

Grandpa Sackter, accordin' to my dad, was called "Moises das Reuter" (Moses the Red Beard). He said he was a short, plump man like me but with a real red beard. Me, I jus gots a gray beard. But Grandpa wanted his childern to go to America and starts a new life. My dad, my two uncles, and my aunt had to walk mos of the way to Germany where the immigrants' boats shipped out.

Crossin' the ocean water in winter was'n easy, I guess. Lotsa Jewish peoples got sick and died. Some of 'em that got sick lived, but not for too longs after gettin' to America. Maybe that's what happens to my dad. He was still sick from crossin' the oceans.

I don't member my dad much. He died when I was pretty young. He was mostly sick or workin' that I never really got to see him much. It was the same way with my mother. When dad was sick, she had to tend to both him and the store. They had had the store only bout two years fore he died. I thinks they felt havin' a grocery business would be easier on my dad than makin' pants in those pants factories.

Jim Dooley said when my dad came to the Twin Cities, he married my mama almost right away. My dad and my uncles lived in a boardin'house in the part of Minneapolis where Jewish peoples lived. My mama, she worked in a grocery store jus a few blocks away. My dad met her there. Jim says my dad had been in Americas less than a year when they marries. After us kids was born, we moved to St. Paul. St. Paul had lotsa little pants shops. My dad did some kind of tailorin' work. Then we went back to Minneapolis cause mos of the Ukrainian peoples from his village lived there. They was lonely for Jewish peoples they knew.

Why they chose a grocery store on the same block as grandma's store is somethin' I can't splains. Jim Dooley says he found out that there was hundreds of these tiny stores all over the immigrants' neighborhoods of Minneapolis durin' these years, not countin' all the other Jewish peoples who worked as street peddlers.

My folks' store was sort-a small. It was two stories tall, made out of wood, and was on the corner of the block. There was only one big room with a storage area in back on the ground floor. This was where they sold things. There were lotsa barrels of sugar, coffee, beans, and ever'thin. It all smelled so good. It would starts my stomach mumblin' jus being there. Back by the storage room was the biggest, blackest iron potbelly stove you've ever seen. This was the warmest spot in the buildin', and us kids loved to sneak in behind it. We could hide ourselves behind the wood that was stacked nearby. Then mama would come to throw wood in the stove and kicks us back upstairs. Sometimes she felt sorry for us when it was real cold and lef us be.

In the rooms above the store is where we lived. There was two tiny bedrooms, a small kitchen, and a livin' room. My sisters and I shared one of the bedrooms. In the other bedroom, our parents slept. The walls of our rooms weren't very thick. Ever night we could hear my father's coughin'. He had somethin' wrong with his lungs, maybe TB or somethin'. They said afterwards he died of the Spanish flu. His constipation was'n very strong cause of all that coughin' and his tough lifes.

We did'n have much furnitures in our bedrooms. Each of us had a mattress on the floor and some wood crates to puts in our clothes. We had 'tricity, but mos of the time we jus uses kerosene lamps at night.

There was four windows to looks out from, one on each side of the second floor. Sometimes I wished we did'n have no windows cause they let in the cold so bad. My dad nailed some cardboards over the window on the north side, to keeps us from freezin'. It was tough livin' then, buddy, not like todays. We had a water pump upstairs, but more'n once each winter, it was froze up bad.

One thing I do member from my chilehood was my father's funeral, though at the time, I mus admit I did'n know what a funerals was. I unnerstan 'em pretty well now. Jim says the year was 1920 and that I was bout seven years ol at the time. Due to my limits, I really did'n unnerstan what death was. I believes you could get cured from it. I can member Sara tryin' to splains to me that papa had died. I jus thought she was sayin' that he was real sick. I could unnerstan my papa's sickness cause I had had the flu jus before my papa got it. Let me tells you, buddy, I was sick, throwed up ever'thin I tries to eat.

It was hard for me to figure out what was goin' on that mornin' when me, Mama, and my sisters were all standin' hand in hand in the cemeterys. It was a real cold day. I was wearin' gloves, but I could feel my mother's hands diggin' into mine. She was hurtin' me, but I did'n say nothin'. I was standin' on one side of my mother, and my sisters Sara and Alice were on the other. There were only a few people there listenin' to the rabbi doin' his readin's. Most-a the people there was some sort-a relatives or neighbors.

I could tell the peoples at the funeral was sad and very cold. Some was cryin', but mos ever'one was movin' round tryin' to keep warm. I watched the faces and the eyes of those standin' round the open pit 'n the pile of frozen dirt. I always watched people's faces, since I was never too sures bout the meanin' of their words. It was like with me and Buddy, my little parakeets. I'd talk to her, and she would look at me, right in the eyes, tryin' to figure out what I was sayin'. Later ons, I think she learned to unnerstan mos ever'thin I say.

Gettin' back to the funerals, I still was'n sure what was happenin'. Jim says it was a day in March. All I member was that the wind was mighty cold. It so cold, it made the top of my head ache. The wind was blowin' right into our faces, probably right from the North Poles. When I looked up at my mama, I could see some tears froze to her face. My own face was so cold, I tried to blow hot air from my mouf up to my cheeks. I wanted to blow on my fingers too, but my mama held my hand too tight. There was a little kerosene heater near the rabbi's feet, but it did'n make no difference to the rest of us. Even the rabbi did'n look like it was keepin' him warm.

Since I did'n know nothin' bout death, I could'n unnerstan why my mother was cryin'. She use'ta cry sometimes when my father was sick, but not too often. My mother jus not the cryin' types, specially in front of her childern. I think I gots that from my mama. When I went to the isstitutions, I never cried, even when I had the bad times. I would jus hurt inside, like I had cramps in my stomachs or somethin'. But no tears would come. Bout the only times I ever cried in my lifes was when the childern I was carin' for in the isstitution was real sick—or a long time later, when I saw pitchures of childern who was hungry or been blowed to bits in the wars.

I jus stood there holdin' on to my mama. I did'n feel unhappy or nothin'. I did'n even feel cold as much as some of the peoples. The others, they kept movin' their feet and hands to try to stay warm. Even the Gabbi read as fast as he could, tryin' to get the funeral over as soon as possible. After they puts the box in the hole, peoples started movin' away, 'cept my uncle, who comes over and takes my mama by the arm, and we all starts walkin' back home.

That's bout all I members of those times. The spring vacation was over bout the times of my dad's funeral, and my mom had to take me back to Sumner School. The problems was Sumner School said they did'n wants me. Said that I was "substandard." But I think it was mostly cause they were angry over what they called my "filthy habit." There was one guy that kept givin' me all kind-a tests I did'n unnerstan. I must-a flunked since they wanted me to go to another school, Blaine's School, where they had special classes for crack-minded childern like me.

My mother, she got into a big fight with the principal bout me changin' schools. The school 'ficials wanted me to go to Blaine's School, but that was a lot farther from the store. I could'n goes alone. Either my mother or Sara needed to take me, and Sara she got to stay in the Sumner School.

There were some bad times at this new school. Since I was new and crack-minded, lotsa kids was mean to me and teased me like kids do. I member they used to sing somethin' like this bout me:

> Bill, Bill, the imbecile
> go to school, he never will
> since he's a fool
> theys goin' put him in the state's school

I did'n really unnerstan bout imbeciles or state schools, so I jus let those words pass me by. But it did finally happen. They puts me in the state school for a long, long time. I don't think it was that I did'n do so well on them tests the psycho teacher gave me, but the fact that I still had the "filthy habits." In the new school, Blaine's, I still could'n find the words to say I wanna go to the toilets. If I did, the kids would look at me and laughs. So when it happen that I peed in my pants, the teacher would be mad, and she'd send me to the psycho teacher, who would march me home to my mama.

Then one day it happened. Since being without a dad, the 'ficials felt my mama could'n takes care of me, and I should go to the states school in Faribault. Jim says these were funny times. Peoples in America did'n care much for Jewish peoples, and if any of 'em showed any crack-mindedness, they yell and scream to send 'em back to where they comes from. I did'n wanna go to the states school, but I never says nothin'. I did'n even cry when they puts me on the train with the matron to takes me to the states school. That would be the last time my mama ever kisses me. She visited me jus once more, though she wrote me letters from time to time. My aunts tol me my mama went to Detroits and got married again. My sisters never came neither. In fact, the only relatives I ever really seen was my Uncle Joe, who was in the isstitution with me, and my aunts who came to visits him.

It was a long train trip to the isstitutions, buddy. I jus did'n know where I was goin'. The psycho teacher had tol me bout the states school, but I never unnerstan mos of what he was sayin'. So jus for peein' in my pants and not being smart in school, they puts me away.

Jim Dooley, he studied how I got into the isstitutions. Accordin' to Jim, in 1917, Minnesota passed a law allowin' for committin' of substandard persons to state isstitutions. They did'n have boardin'houses or anythin' like they do now, least not for crack-minded persons. They had some new tests to tell how smart you was (Stanford-Binet tests), and I did'n do so good. If you was above fifty, you was capable of learnin' and could stay in regular school. Jim says I did'n even make it to fifty.

So when I was bout seven (in 1920), the school peoples tol my mama that I would need to be cared for the rest of my life. Then they took us before some kind of board that judged how crack-minded you were. They tol my mama and me, standin' there with the psycho teacher and the principal, that I was a har'ship to my family, and I'd probably be a har'ships to the community. They commit me, buddy, took away my citizenship, and shipped me off to Faribault. It took till late fall (actually, about half a year) before they come and got me.

Waitin' to go to the isstitution were happy times for me. Since the school did'n want me, I got to stay home and helps my mother in the store. Ever'buddy who comes to shop knows my name. They says, "How you doin', Bill? Helping your ma? You got to help your ma, Bill, nows your dad passed on."

Then one day, they came to gets me. A big, mean-lookin' lady, calls herself a matron, tol my mom she was to take me on the train to Faribaults. My mama cried, but she packs my bags and sends me off. She did'n wants to walk down to the stations to say good-bye, so I jus said good-bye right there. My mama did let Sara and Alice go with me till the train came. I got to wave good-bye to them from my windows.

Morris (the Red Beard) Sackter had four children that came to the United States in 1904. Bill's father, Samuel, was the eldest and had worked as a knitter in the Old Country. In Minneapolis, he worked in the garment industry until 1916, when he opened his grocery store at 804 Aldrich Avenue. He and his young bride lived in the apartment above the store with their three young children. The store, though small, did a fair amount of business. Sam's dream was to save enough money to move to the Plymouth-Penn area of the city where living and income potential was better.

Tragically, Sam had a bad heart, which had been weakened by his bout with the Spanish flu in 1918. In the repeat epidemic of 1919 and 1920, Bill's father again grew quite ill; he remained sick up until his death on March 22, 1920. The doctor listed the cause of death as "dilation of the heart and general weakness."

After Sam died, his wife, Mary, tried to run the store by herself. However, she was not able to maintain the same level of business as when they both tended to the store. Her income plummeted, and Mary was eventually forced to seek a mother's pension for her three children. Before she received her pension, however, Bill was made a ward of the State of Minnesota. Not long afterward, the school board made its decision to put Bill in a state training school.

Mary Masnick Sackter stayed on in Minneapolis four more years after Bill was put away. However, little is known of her life after she left Minneapolis in 1924, when she went to live with her sister Alice in Detroit. It is only known that she got married two years later to a man named Siegel and moved to Canada.

Sam's brothers and sisters, who had come to America with him, all lived full lives. His sister Eva married a man named Chalfen, who would ultimately leave her to raise her children alone. Her eldest child Morris, named after Bill's grandfather, went on to found the famous ice revue, "Holiday on

Ice." Her daughter Sari married a man named Golden, who became a well-known Minneapolis restaurateur (Harry's Cafe, Nanking, and others). Sam's brother Jacob worked along with Sam as a knitter in Minneapolis's emerging garment industry. His brother Louis remained more independent, working for himself as a scrap and junk collector. Jacob had a wanderlust that eventually led him to Japan where, as a self-employed scrap metaler, he lived out his life. However, despite having such a large family, Bill only received two visits from family during his forty-plus years in Faribault.

In the late 1950s and early 1960s, the neighborhood where the Sackter family had lived was demolished. Unquestionably, it had become the most blighted section of the city. The area consisted of small, two-story clapboard houses, with as many as seven, and sometimes eight, crammed into each block. All were weather-stained a dull gray. They ran west from the Mississippi River into the city's first alphabet street and north to 12th Avenue.

These homes were never meant to be more than cheap housing for immigrants who came to America, with little more than their dreams to spend. By the late 1890s and into the first two decades of the twentieth century, the houses were filled with people from Poland, Lithuania, and Russia. All were Jews or descendants of Jews who had been previously expelled from other European countries.

Most of the Russian Jewish immigrants who came to America were fleeing the harsh policies of Russification. They had been made the scapegoats for the unrest caused by large-scale unemployment in their homelands. Consequently, the Jews became targets for government-supported brutal beatings and killings, the so-called pogroms.

Many of the Jews chose to flee Russia, knowing that a revolution was about to occur. With them, they brought a sympathy for socialism and the struggle of the working class. Those who were vocal in their political feelings were targeted as potential subversives in capitalist America. The formation of Zionist societies was viewed by Gentile natives as an act of disloyalty to America. The fact that most of these early immigrants spoke Yiddish rather than English irritated their Minnesota neighbors. The custom of wearing dark clothing and long black coats, with beards for men and wigs for women, also helped to further set the Jews apart from their Gentile neighbors.

The Sackter family had chosen to live in a tightly enclosed Jewish ghetto

on the north side of Minneapolis. The area served as their shetl, a community where they could establish their synagogues, form brotherhoods and
sisterhoods, and operate their own social welfare system through a neighborhood tithe of 10 cents a week per family.

It was their children's future, as well as their own, that urged many
immigrants to pursue self-employment. Opportunities in many areas of regular
employment were simply closed to Jews at the time. They often had no choice
but to start businesses, however humble. Some began as peddlers of dry
goods and notions. The urban peddlers got by with a basket or a pushcart,
but for those who sold in the countryside, a horse and wagon were essential.

Many other Jews, like Sam Sackter, first worked in the Twin Cities
garment industry. Some, with newly learned skills, set up shops in their homes.
The skills they mastered eventually broadened to include carpentry, shoe
repair, and other craft occupations. Every block in the Jewish section of
Minneapolis could boast of one of these shops where home and the workplace were combined. As noted earlier, the Sackters had their own grocery
business.

For Bill, however, the family store at 804 Aldrich would no longer be
his home, his shetl, his community. As a ward of the state by age seven, his
environment for the next forty-four years would be a somewhat ominous
institution bearing the euphemism of "state school."

2

The Bad Times

From the day its doors opened in July 1879, the Faribault State School always had a waiting list. By the time of Bill Sackter's commitment, the waiting list had grown to nearly five hundred. This explains why it took more than six months to get Bill into the state school after his commitment hearing.

As late as the 1960s, when deinstitutionalization policies were put in place, there were still people waiting for admission to the Faribault State School. Ironically, those waiting to get in often overlapped with the many who were waiting to get out. Until 1975, there remained a net increase in the institutionalization of mentally handicapped individuals in Minnesota.

In the early 1960s, some 228,000 people with mental retardation were confined to hospitals and institutions in the United States. Four hundred of these institutions had waiting lists. Yet for all the thousands who would enter one of these facilities, they accounted for less than 10 percent of persons with mental limitations. Many others simply blended into or disappeared within the bosom of their families and communities, thereby avoiding the stigma of being a ward of the state. Bill probably could have been one of the latter had his father not died, for the mental competency board based its decision to institutionalize Bill mostly on the fact that his mother was a widow with three small children. The board simply felt that she would be unable to financially and emotionally care for her retarded son.

When Bill entered Faribault in 1920, the institution was called the School for Feeble-Minded and Epileptics. The local schools did not want epileptics in the classrooms any more than they wanted feeble-minded students. In those days, epilepsy was considered a form of mental deficiency. Epileptics were believed to be educable only in a state school.

The original name of the state school was Faribault School for Idiots and Imbeciles. The School for Idiots and Imbeciles and the School for the Blind and Deaf were under the same jurisdiction—the State Institute for Defectives. The residents of these facilities were considered to be inmates. In their trial placements back in the communities, they were listed as "parolees."

There were times, however, when many of the inmates were permitted to visit their homes. This was especially true during summer vacation periods. Some inmates were even allowed to spend the entire summer with their families. Sadly, Bill would never be among them. He would not leave the institution until more liberal mental health policies were adopted in the early 1960s. To my knowledge, Bill was visited only twice by members of his immediate family. His mother visited once. Records also show that two of his mother's sisters visited him sometime during the 1940s. They were relatives who had family members of their own in the state school.

In all fairness to Bill's mother, Mary, she wrote to her son occasionally during his first three years at Faribault. From time to time, she even sent Bill packages of food and clothing. In 1925, however, when Bill was twelve years old, Mary wrote her last letter to her son. It was postmarked from Detroit, Michigan, where she and her daughters had moved. In the letter, she asked the superintendent if Bill might be ready to come home. If not, she added, could the school be kind enough to send her a picture of William?

The superintendent responded to her letter, explaining that Bill was just too dull to be allowed to leave. Bill, it was felt, needed constant supervision for the remainder of his life. With this information, Mary gave up hope of ever reuniting with her son. She ended up remarrying and moving to Canada with her new husband. She died in 1950.

Although two years had passed since his mother had written, Bill had apparently mistaken some correspondence from his aunts as letters from his mother. One day while recuperating from a hernia operation, Bill thought he ought to assure his mother that he was "fine and dandy." With the help of a volunteer, he composed a letter. He apologized for not writing more often and explained he had "hard jobs" to do in the institution. He thanked her for the money she had sent to him (which actually was a small payment from a life insurance policy of his father's that the institution managed for him). He asked in this letter how his father was getting along, showing he still had not comprehended that his father had died. The letter ended with the following paragraph:

> Could you [mother] come down and take me home
> next spring? As you know, I haven't been home in
> many years, and it would be a good treat for me. I
> would like to come home once in my life.

The letter concluded by saying it had snowed at the school, but the snow had since melted. He asked his mother to tell everybody hello. The letter was signed by the volunteer writer who was not familiar with Bill or the spelling of his last name. It read:

> From your son,
> Bill Sekster

Although this letter never reached his mother, it was read by some other members of his family and precipitated a feeble attempt to secure for Bill a work release.

One of the operators of a Goodwill store in downtown Minneapolis was related by marriage to Bill's Aunt Ida. Ida thought Bill might be able to handle some light work in their clothing and furniture store. Although a staff committee cleared Bill for release in 1941, the institution's administration turned it down. The release plan for the then twenty-eight-year-old Bill Sackter was rescinded. No explanation for this decision was ever given, but some of the staff who knew Bill thought it might have had something to do with Bill's value as an inmate worker. His caregiving abilities were well known by everyone in the institution.

Bill would have to wait until 1964 to gain his release. By then, the boy who had first entered Faribault at age seven was a man over fifty years old. He was not, however, alone in having an indeterminate sentence as an inmate. Most of those without concerned relatives found it difficult to gain release even after deinstitutionalization became a matter of public policy.

The community and the welfare institution were simply not geared to handle the mass exodus of mentally challenged persons back to the community.

I should stress that Bill's mother did not commit her son to Faribault. When she attended the competency hearing in 1920, she fully believed she would get her son back in school. She figured the hearing was simply a necessary step toward doing so. Moreover, when Bill was committed to the state school by the board, she did not abandon him. It was only when the 1925 letter from the superintendent gave her no hope of Bill's release that she decided to leave for Detroit. Her grocery business had never provided her with much beyond a poverty income, and her daughters had reached their age of independence. The offer of marriage she had received and the escape from poverty was too much to pass up.

In the early years of the twentieth century, eugenics was a popular movement in the United States. The established white Anglo-Saxon Protestant population deeply feared contamination by darker-skinned southern and eastern Jews and Catholics who had formed the second tier of immigration during the late nineteenth century. In this light, Mary told her daughters it would be best to consider their brother as no longer living. If it became known that Bill was mentally defective, it could jeopardize their chances of marriage and the citizenship status of their relatives. In the Old Country, it had been much the same. If a child or adult was committed to an asylum in Russia, the family would live their lives as if their relative did not exist.

The designation of state school remained in the Faribault institution's title until 1955, when another institution in Owatanna (which had opened a decade earlier) took over the care of the educable children. During the years Faribault functioned as a state school, its education program was comparable to a primary school, and unfortunately, so were its educational methods. Thus, children who had learning difficulties in a conventional school usually had the same difficulties in the state school.

Gettin' on the train was excitin' and scary. I'd never been on a train fore. The smoke and noise in the station really got my 'tension. I was'n carryin' much with me, jus an old, small suitcase with my clothes and a nice lunch my mother had packed. I could'n wait to eat my lunches. I did'n like the matron that had come to get me. She did'n pretend to be nice, although she was'n really mean to me, neither. She jus ignores me, lef me to myselfs. Even though I did'n want to, I tol her she could have some of my good stuffs to eat.

On the train, there were mens in uniforms with keys. I did'n know whether they were from the railroads or the isstitution. But one of the mens was nice. He talked to me for a while before he had to go bout his work, lockin' and unlockin' doors. Before long, another man comes by with a pail, sellin' soft drinks. He dresses like a doctor in a white coats, but he was black, black, black. Never in my life had I seen somebuddy that color. He tried to be nice to me, too, but I could'n unnerstan how he spoke 'cept for maybe a word or two. So we jus did'n say much to each other.

Mos of the trip, I jus looked out the window. My window was pretty dirty, so I used the sleeve of my coats and some spits to wash it better. Finally, I could see the farmers who were in the fields with their horses cuttin' down the corn, though lots of fields were already cleaned. I could sees the pretty color of the leaves on the trees, too. I saw a leaf blow off by the wind and drop slowly to the ground. I felt like this was what was happenin' to me. I was jus blowin' in the wind, buddy. Even though I had eaten my sandwiches, I felt empty insides. I guess it was lonesomeness and being scared of what might happens to me.

Inside, I kept wonderin' what they might do to me in the isstitution once they found out bout my filthy habit. Maybe they would even cut my pecker off. I jus did'n wanna think bout it, but could'n stop my mind. I even thought that maybe if they cut my pecker off, I'd never have to go pee again. And then maybe I could'n pee in my pants no more, and I would'n get into anymore troubles.

I could'n sleep on that train, but the lady who was takin' me to the isstitution, she slept. She even snored. I farted, but she could'n hear it cause she was sleepin'. I laughed. Don't know why, but ever times I farts, I laughs. Sometimes I laughs so hard my stomach hurts. I was laughin', even though I felt like cryin'. It was almost nighttime fore we got off of that train.

They had a big wagon pulled by two teams of horses waitin' for us at the station. It looked like the horse and wagons they used to take dead peoples to the cemeteries. Maybe they was jus tryin' to scare us kids. It was only then that I saw there was a whole bunch of us crack-minded kids on the train. We all piles onto that wagon 'cept for several of the ladies that was companyin' other childern. They only lef jus one matron to guard us, the big mean lady who was with me.

It did'n take us too long to get to the isstitution. Maybe jus long enoughs to get cold. All the kids was huddlin' together, tryin' to keeps warm. Let me tells you it was really somethin' when I see'd the isstitution. It was bout the biggest buildin' I had ever saw. It was made of bricks, red bricks, and had windows with bars on them. It was all fenced in so the crack-minded persons could'n escape. There was a big, funny-shaped slide alongside the buildin's in case of fires, jus like the ones we had at Blaine's School. I thought to myselfs that maybe someday I would slide down that fire scapes and run away.

I was jus wishin' I could be home with my mama and sisters. To be truffle, buddy, I did'n wanna climb those stairs and go through that door. I could tell all us kids was so scared and did'n know what we was doin'. They marched us into a big room that looked sort of like a gymnasium or somethin' and gave us some inmate clothes and stuff to cover our cots. Some man was hollerin' 'structions, but I could'n unnerstan mos of what he says. I jus follows the other kids. Some of them was smarter than me. Some was even more crack-minded. One poor kid, he starts hollerin' and screamin', makin' no sense t'all. Then he has a fit and starts rollin' round and droolin' overs hisself. After bout ten minutes, he gets settled, and another boy starts fightin' with someone bout stealin' from his clothes bag. I did'n see what happens 'cept the aide gave that boy a mean kick. Then he warns us we all better behaves ourselves.

When we got to where we was s'posed to sleep that night, they divides mos of the kids by their ages. They were a strange-lookin' bunch in the big rooms where they put me. Some had heads too big. Others were all twisted and turned in the wrong directions. A few were hollerin' or cryin' or jus pacin' up 'n down the dorm room. This man in charge would yell at them to shut up or he would kick 'em in the balls. When I got older, I got into some big trouble with this man. He was a real mean type. He was jus wearin' a white T-shirt and had tattoos all over his arm. One of the tattoos was a pitchure of a dagger through a heart with bloods drippin' down. Man, he scares my life.

I jus keep quiet. If I did'n unnerstan somethin', I'd do what the others did. The cot was okay, but I did'n like the toilets. They smelled pretty bad, and they did'n have any doors on the privy. We all had to wash up fore goin' to bed. Some of the kids did'n even know how to wash theirselves. One kid was tryin' to stick his toosebrush up his nose, so the aide came over 'n kicked him in the ass. I heard him mumble, "Dese dumb sons a bitches." When ever'buddy finally got done, the aide marched us back to our beds. It took a while to get ever'buddy into their beds, and then he turns the lights out.

It was pitch black. They had the shades pulled on all the winnows. Some of the kids started cryin' or shoutin'. The boy next to me was swearin', repeatin' the same words over and over again. The aide blew his whistle in the dark and shouted, "You dumb motherf——rs, go to sleep. What-a I got here, a bunch a crybabies?" It did'n matter, though, them boys was scared. I was so scared, too. I peed in my pants. I don't know how longs it was before ever'buddy shuts down and sleeps.

The next thing I knows, this aide with the tattoos was shakin' me, tellin' me I should be dressed by now and to get my ass up. He says, "What do ya think this is? Some god——n hotel?" He was a mean one, that one. I got dressed as bes I could, hopin' he could'n tell that I pissed in my unnerwear. I could'n fine any clean unnerwear, so I jus put my pants on over my naked-ness. It felt funny the way my pecker would rub against my pants. When I was undressin' for bed that night, the aide got mad cause I was'n wearin' any unnerwear. He yelled at me, "You're a god——n bed wetter, a——hole! Don't be runnin' round without your longies!"

It was'n hard gettin' into trouble in the isstitution. It was'n so much if you did somethin' bad as whether the aides was pissed or not. Let me tell you, I learned to study their eyes and their hands, sometimes even how their skin was folded, to know when it was'n safe bein' round 'em.

Once we did our toilet and cleaned our area, we was marched off to breakfast, hunderts of us, with tin plates and spoons. They fed us some oas'meal, toast, and warm milk. Some of them poor kids did'n know how to eats. Other kids would be tol to feed them. As my abilities were good with walkin' and stuff, I gots into the habits of feedin' as many of those crack-minded kids as I could. The kids, they would gobble up whats I put on their spoon, and I could see in their eyes I was makin' 'em happy. By the time I'd get done feedin' 'em, those who could'n feed themselves, my food'd be cold. But I got use'ta eatin' my food cold, so it did'n matter none.

One child, he jus choked all the time and would spit up his food. I tried to feed him once. When no one was lookin', I rubbed down his throat fore I tried givin' him food. It went right down to his stomach like it was s'posed to. His name was Harold. For many years, I fed Harold ever'day. Then one day, he up and died. It was very sad for me. Harold and I was good for each other.

I don't want ya to think all the aides was mean, but I had lotsa troubles one day. It's bout Harold. Harold, he had seizures really bad, and one night, he had a terrible attack of seizures. I was scared and wents to wake the aide who was carin' for us. He was sleepin' like an ol dog, snorin' so loud I was afraid I would'n be able to wakes him. He smelt bad, too, like a tavern or somethin'. Some boys that could talks said he was an alky.

I touched him on the shoulder and says, "Wake up. Harold needs you." He jus would'n move. Harold, he was bitin' his tongue, his eyes was rollin' round in his head, and I knew he was goin' to hurt hisself if someone did'n help him. I pushed the aide harder and tried rollin' him over. Finally, he wakes and says to me, "What the f——k do you want, you idiot." I tol him Harold was in a bad way. "Let the bastard die," he says. "No, please," I yelled and touched him again.

Well, let me tell you, he gets up mean. He kicks me in the groin, and as I bends over, he grabs me by the hair and pushes me toward the stairwell. He's boilin' mad, swearin' at me. Then he gives a push, "Down the stairs, you motherf——r." I started fallin', but he is hangin' onto my hair. He does'n lets go, and he scalps me.

I was hurtin' real bad, and another aide comes and takes me to the infirmary. He has to push me in a wheelchairs, cause I could'n walk. I was in the infirmarys for a long time, and my hair never grows back. The place where I was kicked, did'n wanna heal, either. It was some hard times, buddy. Luckily, my buddy Harold, he gots over his seizure. And he visited me in the infirmarys.

I felt real bad bout what happen. I figured it was none of my businesses to have bothered the aide. I should-a jus taken care of Harold myselfs. I think God punishes me by leavin' me bald the rest of my lifes. When peoples saw that I was bald, they must-a thought, that boy's a bad one. So from then on, I either wore a hat or some wigs, so nobuddys could see what had happen.

Hey, buddy, I had some pretty fine wigs once upon a time. After I got out, Barry would take 'em away from me, sayin' wigs made me look more crack-minded than I was. Barry would say "Buddy, you look like downtown when you dress normal." I still like my wigs and when Barry was'n round, I'd still wear 'ems.

This episode of Bill's life, where he is abused by the aide, took place sometime after Bill was no longer required to attend school. The experiment with teaching Bill to learn to read and write had failed miserably, so the instructors at Faribault School recommended him for lifelong custodial care. They fully believed he could not survive in an environment other than the protective shelter of the institution.

The state school at Faribault was located on a hill overlooking the Straight River, approximately fifty miles south of Minneapolis. It was the area chosen as an outpost by a French Canadian, Alexander Faribault, who had become a prosperous fur trader in the early 1800s.

Faribault's identification as a school dates back to 1879. Many such institutions were founded in the 1860s and 1870s as locations for the special education of "feeble-minded" children. In those days, hopes were high that by working with small groups of subnormal children within a specially designed educational program, many children might be assisted back to "normalcy."

This was clearly a step in the right direction and proved to be a vast improvement over beliefs that feeble-mindedness was some sort of progressive mental disease that would only worsen over time. Yet, even with the greater optimism that such cases could be habilitated, the general public remained skeptical. Many feared the return of such individuals to the community and their likelihood of becoming lifelong paupers.

Faribault started out as an experimental school, drawing some of the children out of neighboring state mental hospitals. The goal was to care for those Minnesota children of "weak mind" who could not be reached by the public schools. Under the Minnesota constitution, every child was guaranteed the right to an education. Thus, Bill languished on as a student at Faribault until age fourteen, when he was finally shifted to the work detail.

Of the two thousand inmates at the time, three hundred were epileptics like Harold. Among the Faribault population were a few inmates of normal intelligence. The presence of epilepsy and the absence of a supportive family usually assured the epileptic of a lifetime of institutionalization. The census of two thousand inmates represented nearly five hundred more than capacity for the institution. As the numbers grew even larger, Faribault took on a more custodial orientation. That a man of Bill's ability could be lost in the institution for so long was not surprising given the institution's size and philosophy.

The main building of the hospital was a three-story, brick and stone structure, fronted by a four-story tower. Spreading north and south from the main building were several three-story residences for the inmates. The north quarters were for boys, and the south quarters were for girls. Bill was originally assigned to the main building's second floor in a dormitory shared by thirty-four other boys his age or older. These boys were supervised by a middle-aged woman whom they knew only as "Charge" or "Matron."

Bill's room was for sleeping purposes only. The beds were so closely

spaced that inmates had to move along sideways until they reached a con-
necting aisle to get to or from their beds. Daily squabbles occurred when two
or more boys claimed the same cots—the cots being so jammed together they
were hard to differentiate. There was little, if any, privacy. Living so close
together, the inmates had no choice but to live with each others' sounds and
smells. Many of the boys on Bill's floor couldn't control their bowels and
bladders, even though Bill had long since quit having the "filthy habit." The
smell in the sleeping area sometimes was worse than the bathrooms. For Bill,
it wasn't the smells as much as the noise that troubled him. Some boys
screamed or shouted obscenities. One boy barked like a dog. Once he even
tried to bite the aide who came to shut him up.

At the state school, the staff made a point about differentiating between the "outside" and the "inside." The outside began just beyond the
arch at the entrance of the school. Down the hill past the School for the Blind
and Deaf, across the bridge that spanned the Straight River, where the town
of Faribault began—that was the outside.

The folks on the outside did not look kindly at the crack-minded folks
on the inside. The rule was that those on the inside should stay within their
campus area, if only for their own protection. During Bill's days at Faribault,
most of the staff also lived within the compound, some in private-housing
dormitories (not unlike the inmates) and some in rooms in custodial quarters. The staff also experienced animosity from the townspeople by virtue
of their association with the inmates, whom they referred to as "those dinks
on the hill."

Life inside the institution was no bed of roses, as Bill's story about
Harold would suggest. Punishment for breaking rules was often severe and
sometimes extremely cruel. Bill's lifelong problem with an ulcerated leg was
directly related to the kick that he had received from the drunken aide. Inmates sometimes were forced to lie naked on the floor and/or were immersed
in tubs of cold water and later placed in straitjackets and force-fed. Deni-
grating and demeaning language toward inmates was not viewed as
particularly inappropriate.

Inmates not only had to cope with sometimes impatient and insensi-
tive staff, they also had to cope with the tedium and the boredom caused by
years of confinement and the paucity of activities. For most inmates, any

activity was welcomed—work, school, church, summer vacations at home. Bill took advantage of all but the last one. Without an interested family, it was rare he could ever leave the grounds.

Bill, despite some experiences of having been personally violated, was skilled at maintaining a low profile. A look at his records indicate there were very few occasions where he merited punishment. On the contrary, those informants who remembered Bill remembered him largely as a gentle caregiver to those less able than himself.

The unevenness of quality in the caregiving staff should not be taken to mean that loving, caring aides were not available to Bill. The fact that Bill emerges at discharge as such a positive and caring person would attest to this. Someone brutally treated for so many years could not have possessed the gentleness and caring that Bill did after his parole. Unfortunately, these many acts of kindness tend to go unrecorded and, in many cases, unremembered. The aides as a group were fine, caring people doing a tough job to the best of their ability.

The state school at Faribault was unique among the nation's public institutions because of its emphasis on religion. Grace was said daily at all three meals; however, it was usually short and quick due to the clamor of the hundreds of inmates waiting to eat. Local Protestant and Catholic clergymen would come to the hospital to hold services on Sunday. Only the rabbi was limited to services on high holidays, since he had to come all the way from St. Paul.

Bill seemed to join each and every group activity that came his way. This included attending Protestant, Catholic, and Jewish services whenever they did not overlap. Bill's deep religious sentiments must have been honed on the hundreds of hours he spent at religious services. Bill was known to have been a funeral regular, whether he knew the inmate who had died or not. For Bill, funerals had the same mystique as any other religious service— lots of solemnity, prayers, and occasional singing.

I have no idea how Bill came to understand death. Even though he mimicked the pain and anguish of those around him, it did seem to register deep inside of him. Later in his life when I saw him distressed by the brutality of war or urban violence, he seemed to feel it even deeper than the rest of us.

Yet for most inmates, one day would follow another with a remarkable similarity. Most were just marking time. They were living lives behind the bars of ignorance and the fears of the community. Unfortunately, there are few records of the stories of these inmates, most of whom, like Bill, were poor historians. Sadly, many poignant life narratives have been lost. Bill's poor recall and a lack of records meant that most of what went on in his forty-four years of confinement will never really be known.

The stories we do know are the few that Bill would routinely share, such as some contained in his forthcoming narrative. But even then, much of what he shares is descriptive. Only at times can one perhaps infer the deeper meaning they may contain. Through painstaking research, a few of the former staff people were located who remembered Bill. Even then, their memories of specific events were few and without much detail.

I did'n have many frens in the isstitution. The teachers got frusterated with me and did'n pay me much 'tension. I was'n too ol when they jus gives up on me tryin' to learn. Nearly ever'day, they would give me a sheet a paper and a pencil and tells me, "Write your name, Bill." I would sit there and tries to copy their writin'. Sometimes if I sat there mos of the day, I'd get my first name written. I don't know what I done, but my teachers would always laugh at my writin'. I liked writin' Bill, but not William. William was jus too long and confuscated.

After they gave up on teachin' me, they had me do jobs. I liked havin' jobs, and mos of the time, I got along well with peoples I was workin' for. On some jobs, I got to move round the isstitution, so's I got to know some nice peoples in different parts. Mos of my frens were boys or mens. They did'n like us bein' with girls none. The boys and the girls, they lived in separate parts of the isstitution. We could be together in church or in some activities round holidays, but that was it. In the dinin' room, they put a big, wooden barrier in the middle of the room to separate boys and girls. They said when we went to dances, we could'n dance with the same girls more than three times. Even when the girls danced with girls, they was s'posed to split up after three dances.

When they tol me I was'n learnin' nothin', they moved me from ol Main Building to the workin' boys' cottage. In this cottage was the mos crack-minded inmates, the ones that could'n learn. Some of 'em had terrible tempers and was always fightin' with aides or with each other. Some could'n say anythin' and jus mumbled nonsense.

One guy who I also saw at Jewish services was named Joe. Only Joe did'n talk. When he mumbled, you could'n get a bit of sense out-a him. But you knows what, it turns out he was my Uncle Joe. Seems he stuttered so bad, nobuddy could unnerstan him. So 'stead of tryin' to talk, Joe jus said nothin'. I found this out when my Aunt Ida and Betty paid us a visit. Ol Joe had been in the isstitution even fore I got there. My aunts said Joe was a stutterer and jus quit talkin' when he could'n get words out right.

I worked hard in the isstitution after I got moved to the workin' boys' cottage. First off, they put me to workin' in the gardens durin' summer and fall time. We worked outside without wearing shirts or shoes. They tol us it was to cut down on the laundry and to save our shoes for the cold weather. In the gardens, the real crack-minded, they pulled weeds. If you was better able, you got to harvest crops. Fore long, I got the job of watchin' over the boys workin' in the garden. I was s'posed to make sures they did'n scape. Hell, how could they scapes? The boys from the Dakota buildin' mostly could only crawls or lay where they been placed. Ever'buddy calls 'em "Deadheads." I had to watch that they did'n shove stuff in their moufs or hurts theirselves.

After many years, buddy, I was given another job pushin' food carts. I had to push 'em from the main kitchens to the dormitories. I had to go through long, long tunnels. Them tunnels was freezin' cold in the winters and pipin' hot in the summers. On this job, I had to gets up early (jus like I would do at Mae's when I comes to Iowa City), and I would have to work almos to bedtimes. The only fun I would have was talkin' to people I met in the tunnel. If I got talkin' to 'em too longs, the food, it'd get cold, and I'd be in big trouble with the matrons in the dormitories.

I did the bes I could in my jobs. It was hard, but I liked bein' busy, and I met some nice peoples. One times, I brought the foods to the Dakota buildin', and I went to the sittin' room to wait to bring the empty trays back. I thought ever'buddy was eatin' in the dinin' room when I hears some music. It was ol Joe makin' music on a mouf organ and playin' checkers by hisself. He'd gotten moved from the boys' cottage not long after I got there. I really likes listenin' to Uncle Joe play. I walks over to him and ask him iffen he'd teach me to play. He nodded with his head up and down cause he could'n speak. Only problem was, I did'n have a mouf organ. So he let me tries to play his for a few minutes each day.

I was lucky. Bout that time they starts payin' us a little money for our workin's. I think I was earnin' bout a dollar a month. By Christmas times, I had enough moneys to buy a mouf organ. But I did'n know how to go bout it. Did'n matter, though, cause one day I finishes pushin' my food carts to the Dakota buildin', and I go lookin' for Joe. But he was'n there. I asked the aide, "Where's my Uncle Joe?" She gets angry and tells me to go ask the aides on my ward. So I goes to my buildin' and asks the aide where Joe was. She looks angry with me too like I should'n have asked.

Ol Joe had died. Hearts attacks or somethin'. Anyways, Aunt Ida and Betty, they comes for the funeral—a Jewish funeral. At the funeral, I asks if I could play somethin' on the harmonica for ol Joe. I played a song I heard him plays once. Never knew its name. But I think it was some kind-a sad church songs. I felt sad thinkin' that I would'n be ables to hear Joe play anymore. The others would miss him, too.

We went out to the graveyards to burys him. It was in December, so it was cold, and the ground was real icy. The minister, he was in a big hurry. He even looked mad cause I was playin' my mouf organ so slow. After the funerals, I gave the mouf organ back to my aunts, only they would'n take it. Says to me, "Bill, Uncle Joe would-a liked you to have it." I could'n believes it. I had me a mouf organs.

I got to know the graveyards back of the isstitution real well, since I cared for so many of the childern when they was alives. When they dies, I'd always gets to go to the funerals. There was lotsa people dyin' in those days, specially the kids with the big heads and ones that could'n walk. Ever'time I'd go to the funerals, I would play my new mouf organ. Sometime peoples attendin' would look at me, like what the heck was I doin'. Once though, the people at the funeral clapped for my song. I know the childern who dies likes my music. Those childern dyin' did'n bother me much cause I know God's called 'em, and they did'n have such a great life when they was livin'. When I goes to heaven, I am goin' bring my mouf organ and play for God and the angels.

Bill often said, "God takes care of those who can't take care of theirselves." He deeply believed he had a personal relationship with God. He believed that as an individual he, Bill Sackter, mattered to someone as powerful as God. When he prayed, he talked to God like a friend would talk to a friend.

It would seem that it was through this immediacy with God that Bill constructed his own positive self-image, although he never really overcame his struggles with his imperfections: his "crack-mindedness" and his baldness (to him, his symbol of his "badness"). As a child, Bill had been unable to see himself in terms of his parents' expectations because of the early death of his father and the involuntary separation from his mother. In adolescence, it was difficult for Bill to compare himself with his peers because so many were severely and profoundly retarded. It was not until Bill arrived in Iowa City and had the opportunity for feedback from many friends that his identity finally came together.

When I was in the isstitution, I prayed lots. There was so many peoples dyin' or sick, and I was lonely mos of the time. If I talked to God or played him a song, I felt like I was'n so alone. I was always tellin' God this was no place to be. He should get me out-a here. I tol him I wrotes my mother askin' her to gets me out-a this place, but she never answered.

It was'n so bad after I started workin' for the preacher and the rabbi. I'd help set up the chairs, puts the song books on the seats—though I don't know what for. None of us could read anythin'. Maybe it was jus for the aides who came to our services a lot. The ministers were always nice to me. Once't in a while, they would ask me to play a song durin' the services. The peoples attendin' the services joyed it pretty much.

You know somethin', I knew what God looked like. I tol the minister this, and he tol me that was impossible cause God was in heaven. I did'n argue with him, but between you and me, I saw him. He looked lots like his pitchures in the Bible, only his beard was black and his hair was long like a lady's. He was Jewish. My beard is gray, and I ain't got no hair t'all, but I am Jewish like God. God was nice-lookin' and wore a white robe. He always had a smiles on his face and would say to me, "Bill, this is goin' to be a great day," and that if I looks for it, I could find somethin' great bout ever'day. When I got out of the isstitution, I members this. It's a great day, Bill, cause you're a free man now. You are a true-blue citizen.

Goin' to church was the bes thing I liked in the worlds, 'cept for playin' my mouf organ. When I got out on my own and lived in Iowa Citys, I went to three different churches nearly ever' weekend. I'd go to the synagogue with the rabbi. I go to the Catholics with Tom and to the Protestant churches with Mae.

There were some really nice peoples in the isstitution. One couple, Mr. and Mrs. Johnson, took a likin' to me. Sometimes they took me for an outin' on the outside. They even once had me home for a holiday meal, though they jus lived on the grounds. Mr. Johnson and me went fishin' once, but I did'n know how to do it. I caught one, but felt bad when its lips got hurt from my hook. Mr. J. let me threw it back. I jus prayed the rest of the time that I would'n catch nothin', so the fish would'n get hurt. Mr. Johnson did'n know it, but I never put worms on my hook, so the fish would'n even try to bite.

Even then, one little fish got caught on my hook. It must-a really been hungry. I guess fishes are lots like peoples.

Finally, when I was growin' to be an ol man, the superintendent talked to me to tell me they was goin' to send me to Minneapolis where I use-ta live. It did'n seem like any purpose then. I had no familys, no jobs, no frens, no moneys. It was jus too late to go, buddy. This was'n the first times either that they talked with me bout goin' back to the citys. Once fore, they said I was goin', but they forgot bout it. One aides tol me they would'n send me home cause I was such a good worker with the handicaps childern. So I did'n know whether to believes the superintendent or not. But they did finally send me to a boardin'house in Minneapolis.

In 1955, Faribault, then called a state hospital, reached its all-time high census of 3,355 patients. Some of the patients were transferred to other facilities, often closer to the patients' original homes. Family members were encouraged to visit and take their relatives on short vacations. The response from some of the patients who had had limited contact with families was positive beyond expectations. Pen pals were often secured for patients without family contacts—like Bill.

In the summer of 1962, an article in the Minneapolis Tribune caught the attention of retired telephone company worker, Hally Johnson. Written by columnist George Grimm, the story encouraged readers to join a "Person-to-Person" friendship program that would put them in touch with residents of the state's mental institutions who had little or no contact with the outside world. Hally and her cousin Grace responded almost immediately, not specifying whether they wanted contact with a male or female resident. They simply sent in their names and waited for a reply. Grace was assigned to Carl, who worked in the dairy at the Faribault State Hospital. Hally, on the other hand, received the name Bill Sackter. "I lucked out, I guess, when they sent me Bill's name," Hally later said.

After several of her letters went unanswered, Hally finally received a reply from a volunteer in November. She reported that Bill was excited to have a new friend and appreciated the candy, coin purse, and dollar that had been sent. The volunteer added that Bill would also appreciate some tobacco and coffee, specifying regular coffee rather than instant. The volunteer explained that either she or one of the aides would try to write responses from

Bill as often as they could but that sometimes other duties would delay the writing of letters.

Hally became a faithful correspondent, even though the responses were slow in coming. When spring finally arrived, Hally, her sister Alice, and her cousin Grace took their first of several trips to Faribault to meet their pen pals and to take Bill and Carl for rides around the town. Carl, typical of men who worked in the dairy, had little to say, but Bill enjoyed conversing with the women. The end of each visit was made special by stopping for a snack or ice cream. Then the women would give each of the men a dollar or two to spend for their needs. Holidays and birthdays were also remembered by cards and a gift or money to spend.

Hally Johnson would also take her pen pal to her home, which she shared with her sister. Hally and Alice would prepare Bill's favorite meal, fried chicken, and top it off with some wild blackberry pie. Bill would eat like he was coming off a ten-day fast. After the meal, they would retire to the front porch where Bill would entertain them with a small repertoire of polka renditions, played on his harmonica.

Often restricted at Faribault as to where he could walk and how long he could be gone, Bill cherished the long strolls he and Hally took. He never complained about his leg. Bill's adaptation to his new freedom, however, had one small obstacle. Due to his many years of simply crossing the institution's yard to go from building to building, Bill was at first frustrated by Hally's walking course, which included turning several corners. Hally said she would look over her shoulder only to find that Bill had stopped at the corner as if it was all just too much for him. But eventually, Bill put his faith in his friend's ability to guide him home again. Although Bill wasn't quite yet a free man, his spirits were rising fast. For anyone who has ever wondered whether volunteerism is worth the effort, in Bill's case, it was his first breath of life on the outside, and he loved it.

Community attitudes and acceptance of mentally challenged persons were finally beginning to shift. It had been documented that some children had made or were capable of making real improvements. The medical disease theory about retardation was giving way to one that acknowledged the problem to be as much a lack of opportunities as a lack of brains.

The financial costs of institutional care were also on the increase. As a result, when the Social Security Act was amended in 1955 to include those who were disabled before age eighteen, the Minnesota legislature saw an opportunity to capture some federal funds to support a community-based care program. In 1957, a second amendment broadened Social Security coverage for the retarded, making monthly living payments available to them to live in the community. Families were encouraged to assume guardianship of persons who for years had been wards of the state.

Those who would leave the institution were among the higher-functioning inmates or were older inmates whom the staff believed would cause no trouble in the community. Public opinion finally accepted that long-term institutionalization could have a negative impact on the developmental abilities of mentally challenged persons.

Bill was one of the early patients considered for community placement. Without family advocates, however, he stayed far longer than many others who were less functionally able than he. Most placements were made with patients' families, foster homes, board-and-care homes, and in county, state, or private nursing homes. Only a small number were supervised by the county welfare department. The department had made only fifty-two such placements by 1962 when the Faribault hospital social service unit began a writing campaign to get Bill back to the community.

In trying to sell Bill back to the community, some of the communications with the Hennepin County Department of Social Service included such references as:

> Although Bill is markedly retarded, he has a
> pleasing disposition, is always cheerful and
> smiling. . . . he is eternally optimistic.

> He smokes moderately, but has no other known
> objectionable habits.

> Most of all, Bill likes to talk.

> He will cheerfully do whatever is asked and will
> take pleasure in the simplest task.

> Bill is Jewish and attends Jewish services. He also
> attends Protestant services with equal interest,
> and I am sure with very little encouragement,
> would attend mass and confession.

Finally, on September 4, 1964, Bill was released. He had been in the institution just two months shy of forty-four years.

When he was first admitted to Faribault, Bill's IQ tested out at 55, or little more than half the intelligence expected of a normal seven-year-old. His last IQ test, taken in 1961, yielded a score of 32, only one-third of what would be expected of a fifty-year-old.

In some ways, Bill was a product of the system. He was taught the life of the imbecile, which he mastered, and he was never prepared to rejoin the outside world. Yet there he was in 1964, back in community, still unable to read and write. He knew nothing of the value of a dollar because inmates were not allowed to have money. Any earnings an inmate might have had, up to a dollar per month, were kept in his or her account book. Once a month, inmates were allowed to go to the institution's store and purchase items whose value they did not understand.

Living his forty-four years according to bureaucratic routines, Bill had never learned to tell time. His movements were controlled by a schedule determined by people other than himself. The days of the week were known by the twice-weekly baths and change of clothes, by sick call, by visitors' day, church services, the Saturday movies, and, from the mid-1950s, by the Monday night religious class for Jewish inmates.

The passage of the month was indicated by the trip to the institution's store. The years ran from Christmas to Easter, the Fourth of July, Thanksgiving, and back to Christmas—when the residents renewed their argument over whether they were eating turkey or chicken.

However, there was one major advantage Bill carried out of Faribault that no lack of education could take away: He was determined to find a home and to be "a regular, good man."

After being released, Bill settled in a boardinghouse on the near south side of Minneapolis. It was an area of older homes, many of which had been converted into multiple dwellings; some light industry; small stores; bars; and several of the city's older hospitals. In 1961, beautician Alyce Cameron converted a former home for elderly persons into a boardinghouse for men who had been released from the state's institutions, most of them coming from Faribault. Bill was one of eight men who occupied the four bedrooms on the second floor and shared a single bathroom.

There were some changes in the makeup of the boarders during Bill's six years at Cameron's, although four or five of those who were there when he arrived remained for a lengthy period. There was Benny, who was a favorite of Baby, the black cat; and Roy, who played with Ginger, the part-collie dog—who preferred to remain in the house with the men rather than outside. While the Cameron grandchildren were entertained by Abe, it was Bill who provided music with his harmonica.

Alyce, a petite woman who pulled her blonde hair back into a bun, attempted to educate the men on the value of various coins, knowing that other people occasionally took advantage of them. In an attempt to reduce the number of such occasions, she often quizzed the men on what they intended to buy during their trips to the nearby stores or to downtown Minneapolis. By providing them with just the small amount that was needed for their purchases, she reduced the total that could be taken by dishonest salesmen. As in the institution, the money was kept by Cameron and doled out to the men as they needed it.

She was as protective of her tenants as she was generous in serving meals and in celebrating the men's birthdays and other holidays. Bill seemed to be in need of her intervention, particularly when she discovered that a nearby auto body shop was only paying Bill fifty cents a day to sweep out the building.

Bill's stay at Alyce Cameron's was made more enjoyable by the frequent visits of Hally Johnson. His anticipation of these visits was noted by Mrs. Cameron, who said that Bill was often ready an hour or two ahead of Hally's appointed arrival. They would take a bus to the Lake of the Isles on the west edge of Minneapolis, walking around the lakes and watching the ducks.

At home, Bill roomed with a man named Harold in one of the four, second-story bedrooms. Bill wanted to work with Harold at an insurance company's cafeteria, but instead he was assigned to a sheltered workshop run for people with cerebral palsy. The fondness Bill had for Harold might have had something to do with the fact that Harold had been the name of one of Bill's closest acquaintances in the institution. At the CP workshop, Bill's task was painting soda pop bottle cases. At times, when there was nothing for Bill to do at the workshop, he would do odd jobs, such as mow lawns, shovel snow, or other work. For a short period of time, as noted, he cleaned up an auto repair shop, working a six-hour day, for a daily wage of fifty cents.

Ironically, what Bill missed most in his return to the community was the full-day work assignments he had had in the institution. None of the community jobs seemed to compare with the jobs he had held as a gardener, caregiver, food purveyor, and chaplain's assistant in the institution. At the boardinghouse, the three-meal-a-day routine only interrupted what was for Bill a very long and incomplete day. There were group walks around the neighborhood that Bill felt were too reminiscent of institutional life. However, he did enjoy the bus trips to downtown, where he had the chance to get an ice cream cone and the opportunity to tour Woolworth's, with its endless variety of consumer items. The toy section, in particular, amazed these men who had never truly experienced their own childhood. All of Alyce Cameron's boarders had practically grown up as well as grown old in the institution.

As new boarders constantly arrived at Cameron's home, some of the regulars moved on to nursing homes. The newcomers provided a sort of courier system, bringing news from the institution. They also brought a fresh supply of Old Rip, the institution's smoking tobacco that was given free to inmates. It was the foul smell of Old Rip that caused Cameron to ban smoking within the house. Her well-frequented front porch became the designated smoking area for these men. Bill would smoke his Old Rip in a pipe, as he lacked the dexterity to roll cigarettes.

As a ward of the State of Minnesota, Bill was one of sixty active cases assigned to welfare worker Leo Kelly, while another 150 clients still in state hospitals were also on his caseload. Leo felt badly for his community-based clients. He recognized their loneliness and isolation and felt that many of his institutionalized clients were perhaps better off than those living in the community without families or jobs. Kelly became aware of the deteriorating condition of Bill's ulcerated leg—for which Bill had already been hospitalized twice. Bill even spent a few weeks in a nursing home, convalescing from one of his hospitalization episodes. Kelly was also aware that Bill's simplicity and generosity made him a victim to unkind human predators.

Twice within a year, Bill had been beaten and robbed. One time, Bill was simply walking the neighborhood by himself, when three middle-aged men drove up in a car and mugged him. He wasn't seriously hurt, but the thieves took his $1.67 and his well-worn billfold. In the second incident, the predators twisted his wrist when Bill tried to explain that he did not have any money. Bill's victimization had a lot to do with the fact that Cameron's boardinghouse was on the fringe of what was fast becoming St. Paul's drug district.

Kelly was also very sensitive to the fact that Bill did not consider himself "a regular, good man" unless he had a full-time job. And unfortunately, during most of his first six years back in the community, Bill was without full-time employment. He found his visits to the sheltered workshop more frustrating than helpful in this regard. After a time, Bill began to drift into a state of both self-neglect and community-neglect. Photos show him with an untreated goiter growing on his neck. His teeth were beginning to decay. The severe ulcer on his leg failed to heal. Most evident of the neglect, though, were the unsightly wigs that Bill constantly wore to cover his baldness.

Finally, in the fall of 1970, Leo Kelly, with the help of others in the department, found Bill a full-time job. A local private country club (the Minikahda Club) with a record for hiring the handicapped agreed to take Bill. He would be assigned to pot-and-pan washing and stove cleaning in their restaurant. He was to work from closing in the evening until opening in the morning. As public transportation was not available during his hours of employment, arrangements were made for Bill to live on the premises.

On October 27, 1970, Bill packed his few clothes, put his personal possessions in a shoe box, and left the Cameron household for a tiny sleeping room above the kitchen at his workplace at the Minikahda Club.

3
A Change of Luck

Workin' at the Middykata Club was better'n mos of the jobs I had had, buddy. Least of all, they was nobuddy givin' me trouble or teasin' me. I works nights after ever'thin is closed and ever'buddy has gone home. I jus did my job. I starts by cleanin' the stoves. I'd take a wire brush and some soap so strong I had to wear gloves so's my hands would'n get burned. I scrubs and scrubs. I liked seein' things clean and shiny when I was done. Trouble was, I got a hole in my gloves, and my hands really hurt from the strong soap I used. They even blistered once, and they had to call my social worker to take me to the doctor.

When I was workin' at night, I'd talk to God. I'd tell God bout I Dream of Jeannie and the funny things that happened. I did'n think there would be televisions in heaven, so God had'n seen mos of the programs yet. I'd also tell God bout my lifes—how I was a free man now, a citizen, and had a job washing pots 'n pans. I tol him I was gonna vote, but not for Richer Nixon cause he was a donkey's ass. I watched him on the television once't and did'n like him much. A guy could'n trust him. He had bad eyes and shaky hands.

Sometimes I'd jus talk to myselfs. I'd say, ol Bill, we got to get you another wig. The ones you got is too tight. Or, what we gonna eat tonights? They would leave the 'frigerator open for me to take somethin' for my lunch. As I could'n cook, I would make me a sandwiches with lunch meats and cheese, lettuce, pickles, tomatoes, onions, ketchup, and mustard. It was a real dogwood sandwich. I'd drink coffee with it. I always had all the coffees that was lef. I did'n clean the coffeepots till the last thing, so I'd have coffees to drink all night long. Truf was, I was gettin' to be a fat man. I was fat, dumb, and bald—not much of a man. A crack-minded ol man, that's what I was. But at least, I did have me a full-time job.

My bosses came and 'vited me special to go to the Christmas partys. I know I was Jewish, but I knew Jesus was a Jew and God was the same for ever'buddy. So I never worries bout it. I also got the night off from workin' if I went. Oh it was somethin'—that party. It was in the main buildin' where they served the rich folks. There was decorations ever'where. They even had a real Santa Claus come. I got to talk to him. He asked me what I wanted for Christmas. I tol him, "Peaces in the world." I could'n think of anythin' I wanted for myself. I likes beer, but I did'n need to ask for it, since there was lots of it at the party. Somebuddy said to me, "Hey, buddy, you'd look good as Santa Claus yourselfs." Must-a been cause I got a big, bushy, gray beard.

I was sittin' at a table by myselfs, actually lookin' at a balloon that got free and was stuck to the ceilin'. It was a red balloon and seemed like a real person to me. I wanted to get it out into the real air, so I could let it float up to God, but I could'n cause of the ceilin'. I wished I was twenty feet tall, so I could free it. Before long, it popped, and I felt kind-a good bout it, like it had made itself free.

When I looked down again, I saw a pretty girl who was a waitress at the club. She was always waitin' for her husbans when I went to work. Her name was Bevy. She was at the party with this same boy. I'd seen him come to get her once't in a while, and I'd always waves to them from the kitchen window when they were leavin' in his car. They would waves back. Bevy waved at me at the party as she was dancin' with her young man. After the dance, she came over to my tables and sat with me. She introduced me to her husband. His name was Barrymor.

"Merry Christmases," they said. I said the same. Then this Barrymor started askin' me all sort-a questions. "What's your name, buddy? Where you from? How long ya been working here? What ya do with your spare time?" I answered as bes I could, even tol him bout spendin' all those years in the isstitution. He asked me all sort-a things bout my life in the isstitution, and we talked till the partys was over. He said, "Ol Bill, I think you're a pretty interestin' guy, and I'd like to take you round and show you the city sometime."

I really likes this boy. He was funny and likes makin' jokes all the time. And Bevy, she was pretty and nice. She seemed like she was goin' to cry when I tol Barrymor bout the isstitutions. That night I tol God bout my new frens and thanks him for givin' me frens and such a nice partys. I could'n waits to see Barrymor again.

On my days off, Barrymor would come. He was a skinny kid and had his hair all puts back in a horse's tail. I think he was a hippie cause he wore some pretty strange clothes, too. His frens dressed even stranger. One of his frens was named Jack, and he dressed like a clown. Another fren was called Bear, and he wore coveralls without a shirt, like we use-ta do in the isstitution, but jus in the summer.

Barrymor's car was kind-a of funny, too. It did'n have a heater, so we'd have to wrap ourselves in blankets when we went out. We'd always go to the stores, so I could buy toosepastes and hard candies. Sometimes I would buy a big cigar and sit in my room and try to blow smoke rings and listen to polka musics. I never could blow smoke rings like I'd seen other peoples do. The polka music I liked was played by the Six Fats Dutchmen and a guy by names of Whoopee John. Barrymor tol me Whoopee John's last name was Wilfarts. When he tol me that, I jus starts laughin' and could'n stop for nothin'. Whoever heard of a names like farts?

Then one day, Barrymor shows up with his camera on my days off. He tells me he is studyin' television stuff and wants to take my pitchures some-times. It did'n bother me none. It was fun when Barrymor would dress me up in different costumes and take my pitchures.

One time, he dressed me up as a riverboat captains when we were goin' on a river cruise ship with his fren J.D. and J.D.'s girlfren. Another times, we were goin' to a partys, and he dresses me up as Billy the Kid, since my name is Bill. I even had a pistol and holster to wear. Then he dressed me as an ol-fashioned airplane pilots and another time as a perfessor. Seems I was always gettin' dressed up for somethin'. Barrymor would take my pitchures with his camera and then show me whats he had done. I'd laugh cause I looked so difference.

Before long, Barrymor was comin' more'n once a week. I had Sundays off and Tuesdays off. On Sundays, Barrymor and his frens had a band, and this band got jobs at hotels or wents to isstitutions to plays for inmates. I got to go with 'em. They would buy me a pitcher of beer and let me get up to dance when the music got my motor started. I'd dance and laugh. Then once, I pulled out my ol mouf organ and started playin'. Barrymor and the band members, they clapped. When I was done, the peoples at the Holiday Inns started clappin', too. After that, almos ever'times they went somewheres to play, they'd ask me to play my mouf organ.

I remember Barry telling me the story of the St. Patrick's gig in St. Paul, where it seemed that the crowd was far more interested in imbibing green beer than listening to some young, green musicians. The music of Barry's Blue Sky Band was literally falling on deaf ears. Bill, on the other hand, was not used to being ignored, so he took matters into his own hands. He reached for his harmonica and started playing something that came close to being an Irish jig. With his foot tapping loudly, he got the unruly crowd's attention.

Bill played with the heart of a leprechaun. In fact, he slightly resembled a leprechaun, being short of stature and a bit on the roly-poly side. The audience immediately got swept up in Bill's performance and, before long, were throwing paper money at him as a gesture of gratitude. Barry and his musicians decided to put their instruments aside and pick up the cash. After that, Bill was promoted to being part of their act. His payment began with a pitcher of beer and ended with a roomful of attention. Bill loved the visits the Blue Sky Band paid to local institutions. He was particularly fond of performances at residential treatment centers for the mentally retarded. Here, he felt at home. He experienced no antipathy toward the sometimes strange-looking and strange-acting children and adults. He knew how to reach them. During similar performances at nursing homes, he could be a little overly solicitous to the elderly. His many years as an unpaid caregiver in institutions led him to speak to less-able people as if they were children. It was delightful, however, to see him carry out his role as a caregiver, to see him take the lead, since most of his life had been spent on the receiving end.

In many ways, Bill was a composite of two contrasting personalities: the shy, private man uncertain of himself in a confusing world and the man on the stage, the entertainer, who simply assumed people were there to see him perform.

I liked goin' with Barrymor and his frens. Most of all, I liked visitin' at Barrymor's place and being with Bevy. I got to do this lots after Clay, Barrymor's first child, was born.

Barrymor called me Clay's grandpa, and I liked this. Cause of my experiences in the isstitution, I knew how to be good and gentles with babies. Bevy let me hold Clay even when he was jus born. I talk softly to Clays and tell him that he was a nice-lookin' baby and God loves him. I sit and rocks him till he goes to sleep. Sometimes, I'd play my mouf organ for to stop him when he was cryin'.

Barrymor's place was really different. He lived in somethin' like a warehouses. It was big. We enters through a side door and walks through a long, dark hallway to get to his livin' quarters. His 'partment was all decorated in bright colors with polsters ever which way. They were pitchures of peoples that were famous in the rocks-and-rolls bands. Peoples like Elvis Parsley and Buddy Checkers.

Barrymor and Bevy did'n have much furniture, but they did have a giant record player and speakers and a television camera right in their livin's room. Barrymor was always playin' music on the record player that would get me dancin'. I'd dance with little Clay in my arms. Sometimes, Bevy would dance with me, too. Sometimes, we would all dance—Bevy, Barrymor, Clay, and me—jus doin' steps by ourselves, anythin' we wanted to do.

On Sundays when the band did'n play, we could go visit Barrymor's parents. I joyed that very much cause Barrymor's mother would fix good food. Barrymor would ask me what I wanted and I'd say, "Chicken on Sunday, buddy." Then he'd call his mama and ask her to fix some chicken for me. Now it was'n all rosebushes. I'd get to eatin' chicken at his mama's, and Barrymor would start tellin' me how to do it and how much to eats. I did'n like him doin' this. Once I got mad and lef the table and went out the door to walk home. But I did'n know how to get home. As a crack-minded person, I could get confused jus walkin' round the block. That happened to me in Iowa City, many times.

Barrymor's mother and dad were really nice. His dad helped me to get some eyeglasses cause he had some kind of store that sold eyeglasses, a topical shop. He'd laugh at mos of the things I'd say and tell me I could'n go home till I played the "Too Fat Polka." Barrymor's brother and sister were still livin' at home, though another sister, Barry said, was a movie actress. I met her when Barrymor invited me to go to California for my birthsday. She had a house with a swimmin' pool. She took my shoes off and let me soak my feets in her pool and gave me a beer to drink. All of Barrymor's people and frens was very nice.

For a man without a family, Bill had wandered into an extended family that loved and amused him, as apparently, he did them. Barry and Bev were still in their early twenties and parents of a young son, Clay. As a couple, they were well-suited to the 1960s: alive, challenging, unorthodox, creative, energetic, ready to take on a world they believed needed some changing. Most of all, they were loving to each other, to their son, and to Bill.

J. D., Barry's closest friend, seemed to be nearing the end of his adolescent hippie phase and entering into adulthood, without losing any of his craziness or clownishness. He would eventually go on to become the national Ronald McDonald. Bear, another Morrow friend, the barefoot wrestler and truck driver, would struggle through life until middle age brought him a wife, five children, and a modicum of stability. Steve, a gentle man and an architect, who like Barry had somehow managed to fall a credit short of college graduation, would eventually, but unconventionally, follow Barry and Bill to Iowa.

This extended Minnesota family of Bill's, however, would be rivaled, if not fully replaced, by Bill's Iowa City family. Yet before this could happen, an important step had to be completed. Legally, Bill's "family" was still the State of Minnesota. Since the age of seven, on that fateful day in which the probate court decided to involuntarily commit Bill to Faribault, Bill had remained under public guardianship.

On many occasions, Bill would complain that he was not his own man, that he was not a free man. After several years of association and friendship, Barry finally reached a point where he felt he owed it to Bill to "set him free." So Barry, almost, but not quite, a college graduate, petitioned the court for guardianship of Bill. Though Barry's request was puzzling to the court and the court's home investigator, the court decided in favor of awarding the youthful Barry custody of Bill. When the papers were officially signed, Barry organized a "coming out" party for Bill and ceremoniously handed Bill his papers with the words, "You're a free man now, buddy. You're gonna have to care for yourself and help me care for Clay." Bill jumped for joy, danced, played his harmonica, ate chicken, and left the party with a contented heart. The good times had come.

4
The Good Times

I was eatin' over at Barrymor's one night when Barrymor all serious like says to me, "Bill, I got to tell you somethin'." He sputtered a little as he tol me he had accepted a new job somewhere in a place called Iowa. I never heard of Iowa fore, jus thought it was some place in Minnesota where he could drive to and back. Then he said it was a long way away from Minneapolis and he'd be movin'.

Man, did I get scared. I could'n eat no more. I could'n even talk. Nothin' was workin' insides of me. Finally, words came to my mouf. I looked at Barrymor 'n asked, "Does this means I got to go back to isstitution?" Barrymor, he smiles and puts his arms round me. He says, "Ol Bill, I wouldn't go anywhere without you. But you are a free man now. You have to make up your own mind now."

I tol him that the good times had come, but only if I could be with my new family. I says I wants to go, buddy, real bad, if you knows what I mean. Barrymor splains to me that he'd talked to this guy, Tom, who runs the university in Iowa, bout me gettin' a job. Tom tol him he would find a job for ol Bill somehows. He also tol me that while I'd be livin' with him at first, he'd helps me to fine my own places to live, bein' that I was a man of my own. That's jus fine, I tol him. I'm a citizen now, and I know hows to work and lives on my own.

The arrival of Bill and his family in Iowa is a story in itself. Barry and Bev, with Clay in tow, piled their belongings into a rental truck one hot, humid August day in 1975. And with a caravan of cars following, they left Minnesota and made their way to Iowa, to the small, rural village of Richmond, just west of Iowa City, where Barry had rented a farmhouse. Bill arrived in a car chauffeured by Jack the Clown. As Bill first set foot in his new community of Richmond, Iowa, he had one small suitcase that contained the sum total of his estate. For two weeks, Bill would live at the farmhouse until Barry found him a room in the boardinghouse of Mae Driscoll in Iowa City.

Bill's fortuitous living arrangement in Mae Driscoll's household is a major part of his story. Mae had worked as a laundress for the University of Iowa most of her adult life. Only after she retired and her husband died did she start taking in boarders. Her house was a relatively small, humble, wooden frame structure dating from the 1920s. It was sandwiched between a pair of similar houses on Yewell Street near its intersection with Friendly Avenue on the east side of Iowa City.

Mae was a deeply religious, old woman, who regularly attended a neighborhood fundamentalist Protestant church. As an added supplement to her meager income, she raised and sold African violets and parakeets. A vine-covered greenhouse attached to the house gave the white exterior of her home some distinction and originality, as did the presence of one of the boarder's 1950 Indian motorcycle parked on the front driveway.

By the time Bill moved into the Driscoll home, Mae was well into her seventies. Age had begun to take its toll on her body. A former smoker, she had difficulty with breathing and, for nearly the last decade of her life, would be dependent on oxygen supplement. She dressed in well-washed and well-worn housedresses, which she shared with her lone female tenant, a retarded woman named Angela. Mae spoke slowly and softly, with a Missouri hill country twang. She was quite orderly in her affairs and prone to penny-pinching. But most of all, she loved her household. She cared for her boarders with the best of maternal instincts. While never hesitant to scold them when they violated house rules, she was consummately forgiving of their transgressions. Her boarders rarely left her, and she outlived more than a few.

The owner of the Indian motorcycle, Kenny, was one of Mae's favorite boarders. He was an emaciated-looking man, with a ghostlike complexion, of medium height and build. With his hair balding, it was difficult to guess Kenny's age and impossible to tell his background. No one knew much about him. He never shared much about himself with anyone in the household or, for that matter, anyone else, even the very curious, such as Barry, Rabbi Portman, and myself. We only knew that once a year, during the summer months, Kenny would return to Denver on his motorcycle for a visit with his family.

Not all of Kenny's family lived in Denver. An older brother, whose name I never knew, also had a room in the Driscoll home. This older brother rarely interacted with any of the other boarders and appeared to have no steady job. He owned a rusted, vintage, four-door Oldsmobile, which when parked, took up almost a quarter of a block. Daily, the driver and his faded green machine would take off and rarely reappear until after dark. One day, he never returned. No explanation was ever given as to his permanent departure.

While all the boarders in the Driscoll household were believed to be teetotalers and nonsmokers, Kenny was not one of them. Although he never drank, he had a serious nicotine addiction. Fortunately, Mae was both poor of sight and smell and rarely caught him in the act. But even if she had, she would have forgiven him. Kenny had become her back-up helper. When Mae was sick or hospitalized, Kenny seemed to have just enough wits and ability to hold the household together until she returned. Kenny would see Mae through to her death in 1986, though by that time, his own health had deteriorated badly.

Another character in Bill's new family in the Driscoll household was Angela. Angela, like Bill, was mentally challenged. Her intellectual functioning seemed a bit lower than Bill's and her social skills had bottomed out. Angela was perhaps a decade younger than Bill, though it was hard to tell her age. While she went about toothless most of the time, she must have had a pair of dentures somewhere in her possession. Angela wore simple, loose-fitting housedresses that failed to cover her protruding abdomen. To an outsider, she always looked about seven months pregnant. Sadly, her abnormally large abdomen turned out to contain a malignancy, though, fortunately, she would have it removed in time and survive.

Angela's neighborhood reputation was built around the ever-present baby doll she carried in her arms or pushed around the block in her buggy.

To Mae's credit and to the advantage of her boarders, the neighbors were comfortable with Mae's odd family, Angela included, accepting their sometimes all too apparent differences.

Bill immediately fell in love with his new family. He worshiped Mae, who filled his lunch box to the brim with sandwiches, salads, vegetables, and desserts, all individually placed in Tupperware containers.

Bill acted like a protective older brother to Angela. Unfortunately, Kenny acted toward Bill in a similar manner, something Bill found irritating. Yet even with Mae's frequent trips to the hospital and visits to her children in Missouri, Kenny and Bill managed to survive when Kenny was left in charge.

The Driscoll home contained five bedrooms, if one stretched the definition of bedroom. Any walled-in space had been converted into an income-producing sleeping room. Bill's room was unquestionably the nicest in the house. It consisted of three tiny contiguous spaces, part of an add-on to the original house, formally an indoor porch.

The outermost area of Bill's space was a sunroom that Mae used to raise her African violets; the middle area had space enough for Bill's bed and a dresser; and the inner area contained a bathroom and storage area for surplus clothing. The apartment was furnished in vintage 1950s furniture of Goodwill quality. Bill's favorite piece of furniture was his Naugahyde recliner, positioned next to his bed in the middle room.

The most-used area of the Driscoll home, apart from the kitchen, was the front porch. At first, this consisted only of front steps with some lawn chairs scattered nearby. Here, the Driscoll household would routinely gather after their evening meal, during the summer and fall months, weather permitting.

Some years later, a railed patio would be added as a gift from Barry. Barry explained that this was a way for him to share part of the small income he had received for his authorship of the first movie about Bill. Bill, an SSI recipient, would have lost a good part of his welfare support had even a small cash transfer been made. No better gift could have been given Bill. The redwood patio served as a community stage for outdoor performances of the cast of characters living in the home at 1311 Yewell Street. Bill was the star of these homespun performances.

Mae's neighbors never complained when Bill played his polka music or his harmonica out front. They only smiled as they listened from the stoops of their own front porches. Or sometimes, they meandered across the street to show some neighborliness and take their places on Mae's porch. The antics of Mae's family kept perpetual smiles on the faces of the neighbors. No one feared her boarders nor did parents shelter their children from contact with these special people. Bill, of course, was the children's favorite neighbor. His gentleness and attentiveness turned them into spectators and participants of the evening porch activities.

Barry's gift of the railed patio tells us a little about the nature of television movies based on the lives of real people, the so-called docudramas. The individual upon whose life such a story is based is rarely, if ever, compensated. In the case of Bill's movie, it was the production company and the stars of the film who were paid well. As a nonprofessional, nonunion writer, Barry himself received only a token amount for his Emmy Award-winning story. Bill also received a token amount, thanks to Barry's generosity, which, besides paying for the porch, went for some new wigs and a couple of future trips to California to visit Barry, and for Mae, a new color television set.

I was livin' at Barrymor's place in the country when I first got to Iowas. I was'n livin' there too long, when he comes home one night and tells me he had visited this boardin'house that had a room I might likes. So my buddy and me went over there. It was jus a house, not too big, but my rooms had a separate door and its own toilet.

The lady in charge was Mae, an ol lady who tol me no smokin' or drinkin' in the house. Barrymor pokes me and whispers in my ear, "Tell her you're not a smokin' or drinkin' man." I tells her this, but says it so quiet like that I won't be lyin' too bad. I really likes the room. It was like the room I had at the Middykata Club. One good thing was I did'n have to climb no stairs to gets there.

But bes of all, I likes the main house. There was a livin' room where Maes was all the time playin' church songs on her phonograph. I likes the church music, though not as much as polka music. There was room for all of us boarders to sit with Mae and listen to music after supper, though mos of time we watched television. I also liked Mae's kitchen. It was small and crowded, full of plants and budgies in cages. But what I likes mos was the smells.

Mae was a fine cook, and when she cooked up foods, she cooked up smells. I could feel sometimes the smells soakin' into my clothes. When I would go to my rooms, I'd sit in my chair, close my eyes, and jus try to smell those smells.

I tol Barrymor I'd like to live with Maes and the other boarders if I had enough money. Barrymor tol me that ol Tom had worked out a job for me. He said I would be paid nearly $200 a month and I'd get some government moneys, too. Fine by me, I tol him. The very next day, Tom and Barrymor helps me move in.

It was'n too long after I got to Mae's that I had to start my jobs with Tom at the Schools of Social Work. Meetin' Tom was interestin'. He was'n like Barry. He'd laugh lots but did'n tell so many jokes or tries to fool me as much as Barrymor. He was real serious when he tells me he's glad to have me on board. He says he was hirin' me as a sultan or somethin'.

5
The Birth of Bill's Coffeeshop

When Barry first proposed hiring Bill as part of a package deal, I had to scurry about to find the funds to do so. I liked the idea of Bill working around the school, since it seemed appropriate that people who were likely to become social work clients could add to the instructional milieu of the school by their presence alone. It was through this connection that I hit upon an idea for financing Bill's employment.

The school had just received a grant from the National Institute of Mental Health for some rural outreach demonstration. Since part of the grant's objectives had to do with expanding the mental health curriculum in the school, I simply hired Bill as a developmental disabilities consultant on the grant. As Bill heard it, he had been hired as a "sultan" to the school.

I did not meet Bill until the day Barry brought him in and introduced him to me. I had agreed to hire him sight unseen because I was desperate to bring Barry onto the school staff. Barry was needed to bring some outside charisma into what was, at the time, a low-key faculty. I had not formed any preconceived notion of what Bill looked like, and Barry had not shared any of the dozens of photographs he had taken of Bill. My only preconceptions were some images borrowed from my brother who was a victim of Down's Syndrome.

When Bill arrived in Barry's company, I was stunned. Although dressed in coveralls and a plaid shirt too heavy for a hot, humid day, Bill was an impressive-looking man. A bit short and on the stocky side, he wore a magnificent silver-gray beard that offset a poorly matched hairpiece, which was tilted a little off center. On his head was a big farmer's straw hat, that is, until Barry's nudge reminded him to remove it. Most striking, however, were his dancing eyes. For a man in his sixties, Bill's eyes had lost none of their luster. And truly they danced. It was as if he spoke with his eyes.

We came to an agreement on Bill's work assignment, and as Barry and Bill were departing, I was struck by the familiarity of Bill's looks. Somewhere, I had seen that face before. It was later in the day that I recognized where I had seen it. He was the spitting image of a Tevye I had seen in a performance of *Fiddler on the Roof.*

To complete the hiring of Bill, I had to move his application through the business office. It had to be done in such a way as to bypass the academic credentials of the consultant position for which he was being hired. Bill had not even completed an eighth-grade education. So I chose, instead, to fill out the form, giving reference to Bill's forty-four years of experience in the field (the forty-four years he had spent in the institution) and skipping the educational background section completely. Fortunately, the employment form passed through bureaucratic channels without anyone noticing, or perhaps caring, about Bill's obvious lack of academic credentials. Fortunately, these were still the days before big universities started to micro-manage their departments.

With Bill on the payroll, Barry and I racked our brains trying to come up with a job for him. After some deliberation, we decided that Bill could perhaps supplement the university's janitorial service, doing things that were not normally a part of the routine maintenance work in the School of Social Work. We felt that such tasks would certainly be within Bill's competence level. And if he were assigned to the day shift, it would give him a chance for some socializing as well.

On Bill's first day on the job, he was assigned to wash the interior windows of a big oak door that separated the corridor from the stairwell on the school's main floor. Supplied with a squeegee, a bucket of soapy water, and instructions from Barry on how to wash windows, Bill was left to his task.

Later in the day, however, we would discover that Bill had had great difficulty in focusing on such a mundane assignment as window washing. There were just too many wonderful social opportunities lurking in the hallway. The doorway was situated in the busiest intersection of the building. Each time someone chose to enter or exit through his door, Bill would convert to serving as doorman and would try to hook the passerby into conversation.

We also discovered that Bill had washed and rewashed the same pane over and over again all day. Apparently, Barry had not explicitly instructed Bill to go on to another pane after completing one. Bill, who was not given to such self-directed thinking, had been content to spend most of his time and energy in people watching and conversing. His window-washing assignment merely provided him with a "window of social opportunity."

Another work-related problem for Bill surfaced even before the workday had begun—how to get to work from his boardinghouse. There were two options: public transportation or riding with Barry. Since Barry was not too fond of the idea of having to pick up Bill every morning and take him to work, he opted to teach Bill how to use the bus. Once again, Barry took great pains to instruct Bill on when and where to get on the bus. Barry had even spent the previous Saturday rehearsing, riding the bus with Bill to and from his Yewell Street address to his place of work at North Hall.

Getting on the right bus turned out not to be a problem, since the bus passed in front of Bill's house every thirty minutes throughout the day. It was getting off at the right stop that proved to be the test, a test that Bill would fail for many days to come.

When Bill did not arrive at the school at the appointed time on his first day, Barry had to go out looking for him. After some time, he found him lounging on a bench in the Pentacrest (the campus center), playing his harmonica for a group of new freshmen on campus. When Barry asked Bill why he wasn't at work, Bill replied, "I am loss, buddy, and nobuddy here knows where the social work school is. So I thought it bes that I sits here till you fines me. When I tol the students bout my mouf organ playin', they wants to hear. Sorry, buddy. We bes get to work now or you'll be lates, too."

Following the fiasco of Bill's first workday and similar conundrums in the days that followed, Barry and I met again to review Bill's work assignment. We agreed that Bill was not cut out to be a janitor, at least not until more supervision was available. It was then that I suggested that perhaps Bill could be taught to refinish furniture. At the time, I was engaged in a plan to redecorate the school with recycled furnishings and antiques. Barry thought it was worth a try.

I should add that furniture refinishing is my hobby and passion. I had decided early on to invest part of my own workday in doing some refinishing at the school. Doing so allowed me to provide some direct supervision to Bill, at least part of the time. So on the day following his retirement from janitorial duties, I led Bill into a room that would, henceforth, serve as a wood-refinishing shop. The room was located at the far west end of the building to reduce any noise pollution to classrooms or faculty offices.

Each day, I would bring a sander or some other piece of equipment and introduce it to Bill. Meanwhile, we scoured the university, looking for some old oak discards that Bill could work on. We managed to find a gold mine of golden oak has-beens. With these in hand, I felt the time had come to put Bill to work. The safest thing, I thought, was to limit him to routine sanding. And sand, he did. As with the window-washing debacle, Bill tended to be easily distracted and would end up sanding valleys in the solid wood pieces or sanding though the veneer of others.

In the end, however, it would not be Bill's slowness or lack of dexterity in refinishing technology that would end his tenure as a woodworker. In fact, Bill completed nearly six months on this assignment and, by impartial evaluation, could be said to have been moderately successful.

The School of Social Work had been recently relocated in a turn-of-the-century brick building with high ceilings and solid oak trim. Located on the bank of the Iowa River, it offered a spectacular view from its northside windows. Previously, the building had served as a laboratory school, covering grades kindergarten through twelfth. A year earlier, the lab school had been phased out, and the building was renamed for its geographical position on the campus—North Hall.

The concept of using compatible wood furnishings with the fine oak trim in North Hall seemed quite appropriate. It proved to be a lot cheaper than using the more modern, conventional furnishings that the university was buying as replacements. A major source of antiques for the school came from other departments, which were replacing their old, traditional wood furnishings with more modern furniture.

Bill and I, along with a new "volunteer," Roger, worked all day on

Saturdays as our big push day for completing furniture refinishing projects. Our goal was to completely refurnish the school in antiques or recycled furniture by the end of the year (1975).

Roger had been with the school only a few months. He had just secured his release from the state prison in Iowa and was being supported by a government work and training program to take graduate courses in social work. Nearly a third of his young life had been spent "doing time." While in prison, Roger's work assignment involved heading up the prison upholstery shop. When I read about this work experience on his student application, I knew I wanted to add him to our small group. As it turned out, Roger was not only an excellent upholsterer, he was a skilled carpenter as well. His manual skills were called upon many times in the months and years to come.

When Roger finally met Bill, both liked what they saw in one another. Despite their apparent compatibility, Roger and Bill made for a truly odd couple. Roger was then in his mid-thirties. He had the hard look of a convict who had done considerable time, along with the build of man who had had lots of time to pump iron in the Fort Madison prison. Yet Roger's heart was as fully developed as his muscles, and one could see the integrity with which he cared for and protected Bill.

Bill was just Bill, a caring human being who truly loved being in the middle of things. He had no trouble accepting the gentle teasing and hazing that Roger would put him through. For Bill, work was the medium for social contact, and Roger was one of the "social benefits" that came with working. As it turned out, one place where Roger and Bill would leave their marks was in the furniture-refinishing shop.

One fateful Saturday, following the varnishing of some pieces of furniture, we found ourselves without any paint thinner or turpentine for our brushes. Roger had an idea. Why not use some paint stripper and dilute it with water to clean the brushes? The stripper alone would have eaten up the brushes. Bill had no objections, nor did he much care. Frankly, I thought it sounded like a reasonable solution.

Roger placed the brushes in glass jar full of stripper diluted with water. He gave it to Bill to put away while I was occupied sweeping up the mess we had made. It was perhaps 2:30 in the afternoon when we left. By late afternoon, several hours after we had locked the door, the hot July sun had pierced through the south window where Bill had placed the volatile solution, driving the liquid to a near boiling point. It would produce a combustion fire that would burn the entire contents of what we had stored in the refinishing work area. Fortunately, a passing student caught sight of the smoke and flames and called the fire department. The building itself was saved, suffering little damage. However, the workroom area was totally destroyed, as were most of our refinishing projects. Our on-site refinishing venture was over. The fire marshal issued a cease-and-desist order to any future refinishing efforts on the premises.

Once again, Bill was out of a job. I had received a severe reprimand from the fire marshal, plus had suffered a good deal of embarrassment for our carelessness. From the start, a number of the school faculty thought that self-renovating the school was a frivolous idea. They could make no connection between furniture refinishing, Bill, and the academic enterprise we were supposed to be about.

The practice of admitting and hiring ex-cons also made some people nervous. Even hiring Bill had not been easy for many in the school to accept. Dealing daily with mentally challenged people in the school's environment seemed like too much of a distraction from what some people felt was the main mission of the school.

When I come to work on Monday, I could'n figure out what was happenin'. There was this big dump truck out front of the schools and a bunch of guys draggin' out burnt pieces of furniture. Must-a been a fire, I thought. That's when I saw Tom. He was lookin' awful. When he tells me our furniture-finishin' shop got burned, I felt awful. Maybe I'd done somethin' bad, but I could'n think of what it was.

Tom, he called me aside to splain to me what had happened. Roger, he was'n round. Then I got worried. Maybe they put him back to prison. I did'n have no job again. What would they do to me? Me and Roger both been in isstitutions a long time. Maybe they would puts us both back. Tom said, "No, it was nobuddy's fault, jus one of them things what happens." I still felt bad. Real bad. I did'n take my cap off all day. I did'n wants anyones to see my bald head. Jus walked round crack-minded. John (one of the faculty), he gave me a cigar to cheers me, but no cheerin' could do it. I felt like I wanted to cry. So I jus sat outside all day and watched those boys carry away all those furnitures I been workin' on.

Barrymor, he felt sorry for me and gave me a ride home in his car. He tried to cheers me up, but nothin' seemed to help. I did forget bout my problems for a few minutes at supper times. Mae had fixed a real special supper. We had fried chicken and corn on the cob. Ever'buddy ate the corn 'cept Angela, cause she had no teeth. She jus buttered up one of the cobs, puts lotsa salt on it and sucks it like it was a big cigar. Kenny finally takes it from her and cuts the kernels off so's she can eats it.

Still that night when I falls asleep in my chair, I dreams of fires. I dreams that ol Bill had gone to hell and Lucifer was burning all the things ol Bill liked. I wanted to fight the devils, but I could'n move in my dreams. I woke up all sweaty and had to showers again before I could leave for work, even though I had no idea what work I could do now that our shops was gone.

Before Monday was over (the fire had been on Saturday), Barry and I had conferred once again on a new direction for Bill's employment. It was Barry who noted that Bill, wherever he worked, loved his coffee. Even from the days when he washed pots and pans at the Minikahda Club, Bill drank the dregs from the large coffeemakers throughout the nights he was on duty. Bill always left the coffee urns last to wash.

When he was refinishing furniture, Bill had had a Mr. Coffee machine filled with coffee blacker than the muddy Iowa River. He drank and drank his coffee, spacing the intervals between cups with cans of Coke. Bill seemingly could and would drink anything in gargantuan amounts, including a variety of alcoholic beverages.

Why not put Bill in charge of coffee for the school, Barry suggested. It sounded like a great idea. Barry even thought of some possibilities for a nook along the main corridor of the school where a coffee machine could be placed. Steve, the architect, would be invited to design the space. This, in fact, was how Wild Bill's Coffeeshop was born, a coffee shop that would later be featured in the two television movies about Bill.

By late Monday, following Saturday's fire, Bill was at his work station caring for the coffee needs of the school.

When Tom tol me I was goin' be in charge of coffee for the school, I was happy. Then I thoughts, I don't know how to make coffee. Tom or John or somebuddy's always made the coffees before. I felt bad again. Us crack-minded persons, we can't do anythin' right. I did'n wanna tell Tom I did'n know how to make coffee, but I had no choice. So I tol him. He says that was fine, he'd get Barrymor to teach me.

Next day, Barrymor and I practiced makin' coffees. Problem was, whenever we would start makin' it, my mind would wander. While Barrymor was tellin' me directions, my nose was sniffin' the can of coffee. Somethin' bout that smell, jus rouses me. I member that smell throughout all my lifes. When Barrymor finishes all those 'structions, I try to do it, but I screw it up. Barrymor los his patience and calls me a nut. I felt bad, but I said I knew I was crack-minded.

Barrymor said, "No, Bill, buddy, you isn't crack-minded, but you sure as hell ain't very fast." Anyway, I felt better, and by Friday, well, I was makin' coffee. It was good coffee, too. First cup I made I gives to ol Tom, and from then on, I bring him coffee all day long. After that, I would walk up and down the hallways askin' peoples if they would like coffee. Lotsa peoples started comin' then. Tom and Barrymor, they had to find a larger space cause we had so much business.

Tom found a larger place, but he splained to me that it had to also be called the librarys. Only certain kinds of things could be done in the university's buildin's and a coffee shop was'n s'posed to be one of 'em. But, buddy, we did it anyhow. Fixed that place up jus as nice as could be. Even had a cash register like in a real coffee shops, 'cept it did'n work. I would'n know how to use it anyhow.

People would come to the coffee shop and wanna talk to ol Bill. I like to talk, too. When we talks, we become frens. I had so many frens in the coffee shops, I could'n count 'em even if I could count. All we sold was coffee, bagels, and donas. I like the donas bes. Had one ever'day, I did.

Morris and Samuel Sackter, Bill's
grandfather and father, c. 1885

Mary Masnick, Bill's mother, c. 1915

The Sackter grocery store, with family living quarters above,
in Minneapolis, c. 1913

The state hospital in Faribault, Minnesota, Bill's home for forty-four years
(Minnesota Historical Society)

Bill with Faribault hospital volunteer Hally Johnson

Shortly after his discharge from the state hospital

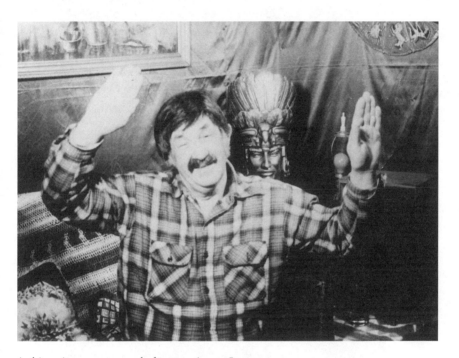

At his going away party before moving to Iowa

Bill's landlady in Iowa City, Mae Driscoll *(in front)*, and Angela, another boarder

In his room at Mae's boardinghouse (© 1978 *Star Tribune*/Minneapolis-St. Paul)

With Mae at a mealtime prayer (©1978 *Star Tribune*/Minneapolis-St. Paul)

Sanding a piece of furniture (©1978 *Star Tribune*/Minneapolis-St. Paul)

Refinishing a picture frame

With his parakeet, Buddy

Entertaining children at a day care center

Talking with social work students

Babysitting Emily Graf

With the Morrows at his Bar Mitzvah

Receiving award from Iowa governor Robert Ray

Practicing signing his name

Arriving at the premiere of *Bill*, a movie based on his life

With two young fans at the movie premiere

Reunited with former pen pals Hally Johnson and her sister Alice

At his last public event, with Tom Walz, in an Ames, Iowa, senior center

His final resting place

6
Life Is for the Birds

Part of Bill's work routine, apart from running the coffee shop, still included some "volunteer" activity on weekends, helping me refinish furniture. We did our refinishing in my garage, thanks to the fire marshal's explicit orders to keep our activities clear of North Hall. So on Sundays, I would pick up Bill just before 9:00 in the morning. We would go directly to mass at St. Mary's Church, after which I would take Bill with me to Halsey Gym, where I regularly played pick-up basketball. While I played, Bill would occupy himself by buying cans of soft drinks for any of the children who had accompanied their fathers to the game. He, of course, would also manage to entertain them with a tune or two on his harmonica.

After basketball, I would take Bill home, feed him lunch, and then we would move on to an afternoon of woodworking. Those lazy afternoons, at least in the mild weather, Bill would spend with a beer in one hand and a sander in the other.

When our sanders were quiet, I would engage Bill in silly conversation. I would usually tease him about one thing or another or warn him about some atrocious thing I was going to fix him for supper. Sunday was my evening to cook, and Bill was my sometimes appreciative guest.

On one of those sunny Sunday afternoons, we suspended our work and headed for the kitchen to concentrate on making supper. I took down a copy of my favorite recipe book and chose a spaghetti casserole I had never made before. Not one to play close attention to directions, I managed to mess this one up royally. Unfortunately, it was too late to try again, so I chose to say nothing and simply served my family and Bill "the disaster."

My children, unfortunately, were unrestrained in their evaluations of my culinary effort. Something about "What kind of crap is this?" was mouthed by more than one of the six Walz children seated at the table.

I ignored their remarks and responded in humored defensiveness by asking Bill for his evaluation of the casserole. Bill's diplomacy, apparently, was severely taxed by the question. After some delay, he finally commented, "Well, I've had worse." I pretended to be hurt by his remarks and immediately responded, "Bill, how could you eat a man's food and say something like that?" Bill was deeply chagrined. He recognized that he had probably said the wrong thing but had no idea how to manage some damage control.

I couldn't help but tease Bill a little, so I began to act as if he had actually complimented my cooking. "So you have had worse, huh, Bill. Where? In the institution? Mae's cooking must be atrocious if you have had worse. Those are the only two places you eat at, aren't they? Perhaps it's at Barry's house where you had worse." Bill shifted his eyes to the floor and said nothing.

I remained relentless in giving Bill a hard time. Then it hit me, the ultimate payback. In my household, there was an infamous caged parakeet. Supposedly a pet, this parakeet had lost all favor with our family, for it had a nasty habit of pecking at everybody, including the one who fed him. The parakeet had such a bad disposition that it had never even been given a name, other than being called "You SOB!" When the occasion absolutely demanded it, the unpopular bird was referred to as "Budgy."

After Bill's remark about my supper effort, I decided to offer the bird as a present for his forthcoming birthday. Bill was unprepared for my spontaneous act of "generosity," but he dared not risk offending me again. He immediately accepted my offer. Perhaps he thought he could atone for his criticism of my cooking by accepting the gift. Bill always tried hard to please everyone, though his limitations sometimes made it difficult for him to figure out a particular course of action in specific situations.

Before Bill could change his mind, Budgy was being prepared for departure in the company of his new owner and trainer. Obviously, my family fully supported my impulsive act and nearly forgave me for the miserable meal. We were relieved. We had ridded ourselves at last of our predatory parakeet.

The following Sunday, when I went to pick up Bill, he wasn't waiting by the curbside when I drove up as usual. Rather than honk the horn and disturb the neighbors, I parked and walked up to the entrance of Bill's apartment. I was about to knock when I looked through the door's small window. To my great surprise, I spotted Bill seated in his Naugahyde recliner. On the forefinger of his right hand perched the irascible Budgy.

With his finger raised at eye level, Bill was speaking to the bird. I couldn't hear what he was saying. From his look, however, it was evident that he was holding a very real and important conversation. I continued to watch with fascination. When the conversation finally concluded, Bill leaned forward and kissed the miserable bird on his beak. Budgy, or Buddy, as Bill would henceforth call him, did the same. Gently, with Buddy's full cooperation, Bill put him back into his cage.

Bill caught my eye and came to the door. He said nothing about his conversation with his new bird. When asked how he was getting along with the parakeet, Bill replied matter-of-factly, "We gets along fine. We're buddies now."

This little anecdote only serves to remind us of the gentleness of Bill's character. My Catholic background made me think of Bill as something like a Jewish St. Francis. The bond between Bill and the bird would be a little hard to understand except for those who are truly pet lovers. Bill related to the bird as if it were a person. Buddy was his roommate and companion.

During Bill's routine weekend visits to the Morrow farmhouse in Richmond, Iowa, Barry always faced the problem of how to keep Bill amused. Richmond was little more than a hamlet, located about twenty miles west of Iowa City, in an area heavily settled by Amish farmers. Horse-drawn buggies guided by bearded, black-suited men were as common as John Deere tractors driven by farmers in baseball-style feed caps.

The Morrows lived in a nineteenth-century two-story, wood-framed farmhouse. This unregistered heritage home was rented from a farmer and neighbor by the name of Giles Escher, who looked Bergmanesque. Giles, his wife, and six children lived next door to the Morrows. No more than 200 feet separated their dwellings. The Escher household was by far the larger of the two. One could guess that the Morrow home had been the original dwelling of a homesteader who eventually replaced it with a larger dwelling as his farm became more profitable. Over time, the Eschers grew quite fond of their young hippie neighbors and their sprightly weekend visitor. The Escher children, like Barry's Clay, loved Bill and his entertaining ways.

On these visits, Bill usually busied himself as best as he could by being Clay's companion. Their favorite activity was talking on a play telephone. Clay would talk first, then Bill. It is doubtful whether Bill either knew or cared that it was a play phone. His conversations would be as real and sincere as if someone were there to answer. The call he most frequently made was to his sister in Florida, who actually lived there in a nursing home. On Bill's behalf, Barry had tried on several occasions to speak with her, but she had always refused his calls.

However, one day, Sara, who had raised Bill as a youngster, chose to answer. Bill was elated, though it was doubtful that Sara had said anything very encouraging. With his play calls to his sister, Bill would continue his conversation. He would tell her about the good times in his life and how he wished her the best of health. Bill was quite familiar with nursing homes and often expressed concern about Sara's well-being.

When Bill would finally get bored with the child games, Barry would find something else for him to do. One assignment Barry came up with was to send Bill to Giles's hen house to retrieve eggs for the family's needs. Giles had offered the Morrows all the eggs they could use if only they would gather them.

With some reluctance, Bill accepted the assignment. Bill's reluctance had mainly to do with his fear of animals he was unacquainted with. As it turned out, he feared chickens, unless roasted and put on a plate in front of him. To hide his fear, Bill would pretend he was not the least bit scared. He covered his apprehension with a very evident false bravado.

Barrymor always wants me to go over to Chiles's and get some eggs out of the chicken coops. Truffully, I was scared of those chickens, but I did'n wanna tell Barrymor this. So whenever I had to walks over there, I would try to get my courage a goin'. Jus bout the time I hits the hen-house door, I tells myselfs,

"Bill, les jus hurry and gets this over." So I would run up to the hen-house door, give it a big push, and shout, "Hey you chickies, ol Bill is here for some eggs." Well, they would take off'n their nests like a bunch a sparrows when you throws a rock. Some of 'em was so scared that they would fly right into windows and walls. I'd jus run to their nests and scoop up the eggs and take off back to the house. Once in a while, I busted a few eggs in my hurry to get out of there.

One day, Giles came to visit Barry and was complaining about how his egg production had dropped off something awful. He could not figure it out. He thought maybe they had some new disease or something. As they were talking, Giles noticed Bill pick up the egg basket. As Giles watched through the window, he saw Bill hit the hen-house door in a flurry and bore witness to all hell breaking loose. He turned to Barry, somewhat chagrined, and said he had just discovered the reason for the drop in egg production.

Fortunately, Giles took a fond liking to Bill and was especially delighted in introducing Bill to some of the finer points of country living and farming. One day, when apprised that Bill had never ridden a bike or driven a car, Giles decided to take Bill for an afternoon of driving lessons on his old Allis-Chalmers. Giles could not imagine any grown man not being able to drive. While Giles's old tractor had definitely seen its better days, it was still a runner.

Giles had Bill climb up on the tractor, and together they drove to a large meadow some distance from both forests and outbuildings. Patiently, Giles went over the mechanics and techniques of tractor driving, explaining each step in detail: How to start the tractor, shift gears, steer it, and, finally, how to stop it. After each mini-lesson, Giles would ask, "Do you understand?" "Yes," Bill would reply, adding, "It's as easy as mother's apple pie." Not fully convinced, Giles would repeat his lesson.

Finally, the time came for Bill to go solo. After one final run through, Giles stepped down and talked Bill through starting the motor. It kicked over immediately. Giles then explained to Bill that by pressing his foot on the pedal to the right, the tractor would move forward. Well, move forward it did. The iron horse pulled away from Giles, heading nowhere in particular and just kept going with Bill behind the wheel.

Giles yelled at Bill to stop. "Put on the brakes, Bill!" But Bill did not respond. He had no idea what or where the brakes were. Immediately, Giles recognized his error and started running after Bill and his out-of-control tractor.

From a distance, Giles shouted to Bill to turn around. Ah, turn around, thought Bill, I can do that. Thanks to several trips to carnivals in Faribault where there were bumper cars, Bill had a modest sense about how to steer a vehicle. Within moments, Bill started experimenting with the steering wheel and managed to get his machine heading back in Giles's direction. Well, I'm not sure if Giles felt this was a good choice either, but he did suggest that Bill keep turning the tractor in one direction. While this eliminated any immediate damage to Bill and others, it still did not solve the problem of how to get Bill to stop the machine. Bill just could not connect the idea of the brake with a pedal on the floor.

At wit's end, Giles recognized he just did not have the patience to wait for his tractor, which Bill was driving in circles, to run out of gas. Giles thought for a moment and then shouted at Bill to drive standing up and to steer the tractor in the direction of a small knoll. By getting Bill to stand, Giles had forced Bill to move his foot from the accelerator, and by heading him uphill, he allowed gravity to fulfill its role. The machine dragged to a halt. Giles jumped onto the tractor and turned off the ignition before it could roll backward. To the relief of both, Bill's day behind the wheel of a tractor was done and would never be repeated.

When Giles and Bill returned to the Morrow residence, Barry inquired how the driving lesson had gone. Giles replied, "Let's just say it's over. I will never again try to teach Bill to drive a tractor, ride a bike, or even roller skate in a buffalo herd." Giles said no more and headed for home.

Although Bill may have lacked the ability to drive the tractor, he still possessed the magic to befriend the bad-tempered parakeet I later gave him and turn it into a companion and roommate.

One day ol Tom and the rabbi comes to see me. They wants to talk bout Buddy (the parakeet). I tells them ol Buddy is doin' jus great. He talks to me, even dances on my finger sometimes. Then the two of 'em gets all serious like and starts talkin' to me bout Buddy dyin'. No, I tell 'em, Buddy is healthy as a horse. But they keeps talkin'. They splains that parakeets don't live long and I should prepare myself cause he could die anytime. I splains to 'em that it's okay. God loves birds, and if Buddy dies, he's goin' right to heaven. I splained they jus should'n worry, ever'thin is okie dorrey.

Rabbi Portman and I shared a concern over how deeply Bill felt about his parakeet. By this time, in April 1982, the rabbi had assumed guardianship of Bill because Barry had since moved to Hollywood to pursue a career in film writing. We realized that the life span of a parakeet was fairly limited and that Bill should be prepared for Buddy's eventual death.

After carefully rehearsing what we would say, we paid Bill a visit at his apartment. Our visit was complicated by the fact that Bill insisted that Buddy sit on his finger and be a part of the conversation. For two experienced counselors, the rabbi and I both felt a little awkward in what we were attempting. We stumbled through our respective counsels, wondering what we were trying to accomplish. After all weren't both Bill and his bird alive and well?

Yet, we could not be faulted for our timing. A few months later, Bill announced that Buddy had died and that he had buried him. Bill explained how he had handled the funeral himself and prayed for Buddy before his burial. He told us he knew just about everything there was to know about funerals because he had attended so many in the institution. He insisted, however, that the rabbi and I visit the grave. He wanted Rabbi Portman to offer a prayer for Buddy. The rabbi graciously complied.

Earlier, Rabbi Portman and I had decided that if anything should happen to Buddy, we would replace him with another bird. So when Buddy finally did die, we immediately started checking out the three pet stores. In the course of these visits, the idea came to the rabbi that perhaps Bill's next bird should be a talking bird, since Bill so enjoyed talking to his pet roommate. Why not buy one that could talk back?

Our shopping tour yielded only one talking bird among the city's pet stores. The bird, however, was not cheap. We tried to soft-sell the pet store owner to reduce the price, but she would not go any lower than $300. It so happened that the rabbi had had the foresight to develop a fund of sorts in the synagogue in Bill's name. This was to ensure that the few dollars that might come Bill's way would not jeopardize his eligibility for a small, supplemental Social Security check he received monthly. There was just enough money in this fund to buy the parrot.

The following weekend, Rabbi Portman and I delivered the bird. Bill was delighted. Within minutes, he had the bird out of the cage and perched on one of his fat, wrinkled fingers. The bird, however, was a little intimidated by his new surroundings and remained mute. The bird's failure to speak mattered little to Bill, who kept up a steady one-sided conversation with his new roommate.

The following day, the rabbi drove to the East Coast for a two-week vacation. In his absence, I made several visits to Bill's apartment to check on how the bird and he were getting along. On these occasions, I was accompanied by a colleague from the social work school, also a good friend of Bill's, by the name of John Craft.

Bill explained that he had named his new bird "Rabbi" after his benefactor and conservator. It seemed that "Rabbi" was making excellent progress and had a real talent for mimicry. John, who had earlier served as interim conservator to Bill, loved to tease and joke with his friends. During one of our visits to check on the parrot, John happened upon a copy of a pamphlet that had been sent to Bill by an organization called "Jews for Jesus." Calling attention to the pamphlet, John started teasing Bill about his questionable behavior as a Jew getting materials on Jesus. Bill replied that it was okay. There was only one God, and he loved everybody—Jews, Jesus Jews, Christians, and birds.

Anyway, John was struck with an idea he could not resist. He wanted to teach the bird how to say "Jews for Jesus," knowing how shocked Rabbi Portman would be when he returned and heard what his expensive purchase had produced. (The rabbi was not even aware that Bill had named his new bird after him.) It took nearly two full weeks to teach the bird to say "Jews for Jesus," but Rabbi did manage to learn the phrase. John, who had trained as an experimental psychologist, had made a tape recording of the three words and had Bill play the tapes to Rabbi for at least two hours every night. The day after the rabbi's return from his vacation, John and I arranged for him to visit Bill in order to check on things. We entered the little apartment and waited for Bill to bring out the parrot. For the first half-hour, Rabbi did not even attempt a "Polly want a cracker." This did not bother Bill in the least, but it was driving John crazy. John desperately wanted to see the rabbi's reaction to his Pavlovian experiment.

John, unable to contain himself any longer, finally asked Bill if the "damn bird" didn't talk. Before Bill could answer, the parrot recognizing John's voice from the tape recording burst out, "Jews for Jesus, Jews for Jesus, Jews for Jesus." Rabbi Portman could not believe his ears. Then looking at John and I, he guessed what was going on. He started to laugh, John followed, then myself, then Bill, who didn't get the joke but laughed anyway. Even our fine-feathered friend mimicked, with its own version of our laughter.

But sadly, the feathered Rabbi's tenure with Bill proved to be short-lived. About six weeks after the parrot's arrival, Mae Driscoll asked her handyman, Kenny, to go check on the parrot and make sure his cage was clean. When Kenny arrived, it was evident that Rabbi's cage was long overdue for a thorough wash down. Reluctantly, Bill let Kenny carry out his assignment and went to the door of his apartment to look out on the street.

As Kenny opened the cage, the parrot instinctively headed for the open door and out to freedom. He landed in the old oak tree located in the middle of Mae's yard. Before either Bill or Kenny could react, Rabbi headed south and was never seen again. Bill, of course, was heartbroken over his second loss in six weeks. Yet, he explained that he was happy that Rabbi was "free" because he knew what it was like to be locked up for so many years. Now both he and the parrot were free and could go where they pleased.

7

Every Buddy's Bill

I sure was lucky. I had lots of frens, many good buddies. My bes buddies was Barrymor and Bevy. Barrymor was always funny and tellin' me how to lives. He never liked my wigs and made me wear my hats instead. He let me wear wigs after Mr. Executive (a Des Moines, Iowa, coiffeur) made me one to match my beard.

Barrymor and me did lotsa things in our lives. We played music together, went to dances, went on riverboats, went to the hospitals to get Clay and once to prays for little Zoe (Barry's daughter, born several years after Clay).

Barrymor could play the mouf organ, the pianos, and the guitar. He could sing and dance. He took pitchures and made his own televisions. Barrymor could do mos ever'thin.

Barrymor would take me to K-Mart for shoppin'. I member one time I needed some work shoes, only I got two different-size feets. So Barrymor, he measures each foot and opens difference boxes till he gets two that works. That way I only had to pay for one pair of shoes. Barrymor was a smart man.

Clay and Zoe was Barrymor and Bevy's kids, and they called me Grandpa Bill. I never had any childern, so I loved 'em like they was my own. I member once when Zoe got real sick they put her in the hospital. They said she could'n hear nothin' or speak or anythin'. They would'n let me visit, cause they said I was'n real family. I was mad. Zoe and me was buddies. I wanted to pray over her like the preachers do on television. I tol Barrymor they should lets me see her. So he talks to the doctor, and finally, they let me see her. When I got in that door, I jus dropped to my knees and started prayin' to Jesus. When I got up and went to see her, her eyes opened up, and she said my name. She was too little to talks much more than that. Barry said it was a miracle.

Tom, he was my buddy, too. He run the university where I had my coffee shop. Ever Sunday, he would take me to the Catholic church and then to his house to work on furnitures. I liked workin' on furnitures cause Tom would give me a beer and laugh at mos ever'thin I'd say. It was Tom who give me the coffee shop job after our finishin' shop got burned. Tom's wife, Lisa, was nice to me, jus like Bevy. She was a good cook. I liked it better when she cooked than when Tom cooked. Tom was always havin' troubles with his cookin'.

I knew Tom was the boss of the university, so I brought him coffee all day long. When I bring him the coffee, I'd sit down in his office and we'd talk some. He'd ask how was business, and I'd answer, "Business is real good." Then he says, "Maybe I'd better get back since peoples was probably waitin' for me." I'd leave, but when things got slow I'd take ol Tom another cup.

When peoples started askin' me to come visit them in difference places, mostly it was Tom or John that took me since Barrymor was in Hollywoods at the time. I went ever'where. I saw lotsa places in the United States of Americas. Once't I even went to Canada.

Some weekends, Tom would be out of town, so's I would go and visit ol John Crass's (John Craft's) place. He had a real nice house with his own lake. Sometimes he'd take me down fishin' in his pond. Mos of the time, we'd go visit a little boy who could'n walk or talk. He was all shriveled up and tied to his wheelchair. I membered boys like him in the isstitution, so I knew what to do. Anyway, I called him "little buddy" 'n we became frens. Whenever I would visit at John's, I would ask if I could go see my little buddy. He and me, we had our pitchures taken. I still gots a copy of it in my scrapbooks.

I liked John lots. He was sort-a fat, like me. He liked eatin' lots and drinkin' beer. Man, could he drink beer. He'd sit in one of those big recliners, 'n I sat in the other in his livin' room. And we'd have us a couple of beers 'n watch the footballs on the TV. John, he teased me lots, but I did'n mind cause we was buddies. He'd say to me, "Bill, you can't have brains and hair both, but seems to me you ain't got much of neither."

After Barrymor went to Hollywoods, it was John that helped me out with my money and stuff till when the rabbi took over. Now, Rabbi Portman, he was always a big help to me. He'd come over to Mae's ever week to see bout my money and my needs. He'd stop 'n talk to Mae, Kenny, and even Angela. Ever'buddy liked the rabbi.

Once in a whiles, Rabbi Portman checks out my closets. He wanted to make sure I had clothes for work. I tol him I had lotsa clothes, but he'd still make me go to the stores with him to buy extras. Never wore mos of what he bought. I like my regular clothes. My job was'n so dirty that I needed to change ever'day, but I always changed least once a week. To smell good, I would shower ever night after supper.

Ever Friday nights and Saturday mornin's, Rabbi Portman would come by to takes me to synagogue. I liked goin' to synagogues cause the peoples there was Jewish and mos of 'em was my frens. They liked it when I spoke in the services. When the rabbi read from the Jewish Bibles, some of the ol peoples would answer. Mos of the time, I would answer, too. I did'n know how to speak Jewish exactly, but I could make the right sounds. The peoples round me seemed to think that was good enough for them. Rabbi Portman, he'd smile when I talks in Jewish. I knew he was happy that I was helpin' him out.

The rabbi got married when he was watchin' over me. His wife, Gail, was young like Bevy, and she was my fren, too. They would invite me for dinner sometimes and cook me good foods. One times, the rabbi, he bought me a new bird when Buddy died. This was a big parakeet that knew how to talks. I named him Rabbi after Rabbi Portman. John and Tom, they helped teach it to talks. They taught it to say, "Jews for Jesus." to makes the rabbi happy. It must-a made him happy cause he sure did laugh when he heard Rabbi say, "Jews for Jesus."

My other buddy, his name was John, too. Why he (John Anders) was fatter than ol John Crass and smoked cigars. His office was next door to the coffee shops, so I would stop by to see him when nobuddy come for coffee. John would give me a cigar, and we would smokes together. He try to teach me to blow smoke rings, but I never learns. John was bes smoke-ring blower I ever saw.

There were two Johns in Bill's life, both faculty members at the School of Social Work. John Anders was the first one Bill got acquainted with. John truly touched the scales at a level of obesity, although his weight was known to fluctuate between 150 and 300 pounds within a matter of months. Anders was a true genius with an IQ that pushed the 200 mark. His complex personality was evident to all who knew him. He did not have any problem identifying the absurdities of life, nor did he hesitate to point them out to anyone who would listen. When he ran out of willing ears, there was always Bill who would listen.

John, I believe, found the cast of characters in the school interesting, Bill included. He placed us all somewhere on his "ship of fools." I think at a deep level he really liked Bill, though mostly he related to him in a teasing way. John was inclined toward a love-hate relationship with the world. At times, Bill could be the object of John's disdain, while at other times, he served as his Sancho Panza. John frequently attacked the rest of us for treating Bill as if he were some housebroken, loyal puppy.

Bill's relationship to John Craft was more conventional. Craft was his guardian for a short time in 1982, after Barry moved to Hollywood. Bill would get into quarrels with him about how he should spend his money. As conservator, John received Bill's SSI check in the mail every month and kept a close eye on Bill's spending habits. Bill always had some conflicts with those who had authority over him. John would die about seven years after Bill, but oddly in much the same manner. Both would die of heart-related conditions in their sleep.

One of my favorite frens was Debsy (Debbie). She worked at the synagogues and the students center, Hill House (Hillel). She was real nice, and when her boyfrens comes, we would all go to movies together. Sometimes they took me to see a movie bout Laurel and Hardy, my favorites. Debsy was a dancer and went to the Schools of Social Work to study. Jim, her boyfrens, was from somewheres. My mind is a rock. I don't member jus where. I knows he did'n live in Iowa Citys. You can jus ask Jim hisself.

While most of Bill's friends were men, there were some women who figured prominently in his life, in addition to Debbie Pava, Gail Portman, and Bev Morrow. Another female friend was a Catholic nun, Eleanor Anstey, who was serving on the School of Social Work faculty at the time. Eleanor was frequently Bill's advocate with the director of the school, who replaced me when I resigned in 1978. The director, Dr. Ruth Brandwein, was at first a little uncertain about Bill and the role he filled in the school. Bill, however, quickly won over the new director, and in turn, she became the new recipient of personal coffee deliveries to her office.

Bill also got along with the young mothers whose children attended the Early Childhood Education Center in North Hall. Although Bill knew only a few of the mothers by name, he was invited into the homes of many. He would be invited for a meal or sometimes for a party when the children celebrated a birthday or when there was a religious holiday (Jewish and non-Jewish). Bill was an especially popular guest on the Bar Mitzvah circuit, since he himself had only recently celebrated his own Bar Mitzvah. We would often tease Bill about women and when he was going to get married. His reply was always the same: "I would rather marry a horse."

One woman whom Bill got to know well was Rosalie Rose, a woman he met through the synagogue. Rosalie was the owner of a small business enterprise known as "Balloons over Iowa." Her enterprise included operating a colorful circus wagon in the promenade of the only shopping mall (at the time) in Iowa City. From her wagon, Rosalie sold balloons to passing children and their parents. Aware of Bill's magnetism with children and his love of costume, she employed him on Saturday afternoons to hawk balloons in a clown costume. Oddly enough, we knew about this activity only by word of mouth since Bill had never chosen to reveal his moonlighting occupation to those of us at the school. Bill came to know a good many children through this Saturday afternoon job. I believe the majority of Iowa City's children knew him by name.

Among Bill's buddies were his Yewell Street family, who more or less have already been introduced. Yet there must have been countless others we know very little about. One example, would be the bus drivers and the regulars who rode the bus downtown. Before long, they all knew Bill's name and were not shocked when he treated them to a little harmonica music during their commute. He greeted everyone who entered the bus by sharing with them his standard greeting of the day: "God sure has given us a nice day" or "You are looking good today." According to one driver, his bus became a bus full of smiling passengers, largely as result of Bill's immense positive energy and antics.

I also recall the time Rabbi Portman gave me tickets to take Bill to an Iowa Hawkeye basketball game. As a non–ticket holder, I was eager to go and took great pains to make Bill feel comfortable in accompanying me. But it was only as we made our way to our seats that I discovered that half the town knew Bill and that he had attended dozens of games previously with the rabbi.

To test a theory about Bill's recognition in the greater Iowa City area, I brought three pictures with me to a neighboring town where I had been invited to speak to the Rotary Club. The three pictures I brought included one of Bill, one of the president of the University of Iowa, and one of our football coach. That evening, I showed each of the pictures to my audience and asked which faces they recognized. Well, Bill's face was the most recognized, the coach's face came in second, and the university president came in third. This, of course, occurred not long after Bill's life had been portrayed in the television movie.

Bill's activities—which ranged from his work in the school and moonlighting at the mall to his attendance at many area churches, his life in the boardinghouse, and his presence at an endless number of parties—each produced a large network of friendships and associations. There were times when Bill had to juggle as many as three invitations in a single evening. He would orchestrate his drivers and hosts to get him from one place to another with a minimum of disruption. Bill somehow managed to find his way through these multiple demands without offending anyone.

Friends, as Bill said many times, were the basis of his "good life." He had done immensely well for himself in building a network of caring people. He truly did experience the good life in those final years of his life. And during his long years in the institution, he may have had even a richer life than we have credited him with.

8

Activities of Daily Loving

In those first years in Iowa, before fame would claim part of Bill's life, his routines were built around his job in the coffee shop. He would rise with the dawn, already fully dressed, have a modest breakfast with Mae, and, within minutes, head for the bus stop. Since Bill could not tell time, he would wait out on the curb as long as it took for the bus to arrive.

Bill's habits and routines were designed to help him compensate for what he could not do himself. For example, he would shower in the evening, dress for work, and then sit back in his overstuffed chair and go to sleep. This way, he would be ready for work when he woke up and could avoid being late.

Actually, Bill's workday was not supposed to begin until 8:00 A.M. On most days, he arrived at North Hall by 6:30 in the morning. This meant he would have to catch the first bus of the day that passed his house. As I would eventually discover, Bill left early so he could be at the door of the school when the first children were dropped off at the Early Childhood Education Center.

When I first came to North Hall, I was distressed by the many scenes of parents leaving the children at the day care center. The tears of separation had become an inevitable part of the process for many children. They would scream and cry not to be left by the harried and hurried parents who were anxious to get to work or class on time.

Then one day, I happened to see Bill at his self-assumed post of doorman for these children. As the cars drove up, the children would spot Bill and start hollering to him. He would come forward to shake their hands, telling them how nice they looked that day. Any tears or recriminations experienced by the children disappeared with Bill's presence, much to the relief of parents. It is little wonder that Bill became a regular guest in many of these children's home. Many parents were grateful for what Bill had done to reduce the separation anxieties their children had felt at those moments.

It was only after the last of these children had been dropped off that Bill would "put the coffee on." The rest of his day, he would spend in seeking out social opportunities with his friends. At least once a morning, usually after filling my coffee cup for the second time, Bill would wander down to the Early Childhood Education Center, located on the second floor of our building. He would look in on the classroom activities of the moment and wait to be invited in. Inevitably, the teacher would ask him in. Given this daily disruption, the teacher began taking Bill and the children on a trip upstairs. Most of the time, it meant a trip to Wild Bill's Coffeeshop. As part of their regular coffee shop visit, the children would sit with Bill on a big, built-in lounge sofa just outside the coffee shop and listen to Bill play his harmonica. The children would tap their feet or jump up and start dancing if Bill were playing one of his livelier polka tunes. After a song or two by Bill, the teacher would read a story to the children. Bill would sit and listen intently to these stories with the same rapt attention as the children. When story time ended, the children would return to their classroom and prepare for their naps. The visit with Bill had left them contented. With the children gone, Bill would once again wander the corridors looking for friends, old or new.

Although Bill could not tell time, his stomach told him when it was lunchtime. Thus, when noon arrived, Bill would bring out his big, black-metal lunch box and lay out his treasures on one of the large, round oak tables in the coffee shop. His treasures would include meat sandwiches, at least two, a jar of some kind of vegetable, a similar-sized jar of applesauce, and more than one cookie or dessert alternative.

Bill preferred to eat in the company of whomever was in the coffee shop at the time, opening his lunch box at one of his customers' tables.

According to his doctor's instructions, Bill would also use the lunch period as a time to rest his foot and ulcerated leg, so a second chair was borrowed to cradle his bad leg.

During lunchtime, conversation with Bill would be limited. He usually strung together a bunch of clichés about the weather, politics (about which he was totally confused), and food. In most instances, it would be the table companion that would tender the questions. Bill would answer to the best of his ability. Whatever words flowed from Bill's mouth, they would be upbeat. Bill's favorite expression was something about God giving us a nice day again. It did not matter to Bill if it was raining outside or 20 degrees below zero, it was always a nice day.

In the afternoon, Bill again would take to wandering the halls. He would stop and talk to Eleanor, Roger, myself, or one of the Johns. These were the people he knew who would not be irritated by his frequent intrusions. He probably spent most of his time with John Craft, who never seemed to tire of his company. Bill served as a kind of escape valve for John's personal and job-related frustrations.

Bill had an uncanny ability to sense when someone—faculty, student, or staff—was troubled. Rather than avoid them, Bill tried to engage them. It was as though he had some sort of psychic sense about troubled persons and wanted to help them out of their troubles, which most of the time he managed to do. His smile, simplicity, and sincerity were disarming to most of us.

When the faculty were engaged in committee meetings of one kind or another, Bill would be there with his coffeepot. He would often sit outside the door of the meeting room until the session ended. And if he sensed the rise of tensions or conflict in any of these sessions, he would start playing his harmonica. This would become a signal to us that Bill was letting us know it was time to assess our feelings and emotions. Many a conflict situation was kept from escalating by the sounds of the "Too Fat Polka."

Bill especially liked when outside visitors came to the School of Social Work, since more often than not, they would spend time in his shop. The coffee shop had become a kind of showpiece for visitors, plus a convenient place to leave them between appointments. Whenever Bill was introduced to visitors, he would make it a point to keep them entertained until their official hosts returned.

One time, we had a group of students from six different countries seated at a coffee shop table enjoying cups of Bill's brew. They were part of an official international exchange program the school administered. Each foreign student was introduced to Bill by name and by country. Jokingly, they were told that Bill had command of every language in the world. Bill, of course, nodded that this was correct. Each student was then asked to speak to him in his or her native tongue. Bill, without a moment's hesitation, responded back to each in that "tongue." He spoke with perfect pitch and rhythm, even though his words carried no literal meaning. Yet the conviction with which he spoke his gibberish left the students puzzled. Perhaps he was, after all, speaking their language. Only later did we explain to our foreign guests the nature of the joke.

On another occasion, we had the visit of a black matriarch from a Garifuna village in Honduras. Her name was Mama Matilde (Alvarez). Mama Matilde was the mother of a young man I had raised in the United States at her request. I had met the Alvarez family during my stint as director of the Peace Corps in Honduras in the early 1960s. This was Matilde's first visit anywhere outside her village. Matilde had been invited to visit the School of Social Work by a local businessman, Mace Braverman, who had gone to Honduras with me and his son the previous year. Matilde, like other visitors, was left in Bill's company when she was not being shown around the campus.

On the second day of her visit, Mama Matilde was left in Bill's charge for most of the morning. According to eyewitnesses, Matilde and Bill carried on an endless conversation in her Garifuna language. The witnesses stated that neither of them gave the slightest indication that one did not fully understand the other. Perhaps they did manage to communicate. It was evident to all who witnessed them that they were "communicating" at some level.

This reminds me of the many occasions in which Bill and I would speak "Minnesotan" to one another. We would make up words and sentences that sounded Swedish just for the fun of it. The students, whom we often used as the audience for our charade, were never quite certain whether we were actually speaking Swedish or not. Bill's ability to speak gibberish seemed to give him some added self-confidence. No matter what social exchange took place, he would have some sort of reply.

Like many persons with intellectual deficiencies, Bill struggled with organizing and sharing his thoughts in words. He had learned over the years to compensate for his deficits by giving impressions of understanding or by finessing his replies. There is always the possibility, however, that he simply understood a meaning deeper beyond the literal translation of words.

For example, if one asked Bill what he thought about the president's policies on a given issue, he would often reply, "Haven't given it much thought, buddy. What do you think?" Or if someone asked, "How you feeling, Bill?" he would answer, "Never felt better'n my life. Jus like downtowns." He had learned the common technique of constructing his answers out of the other person's questions, merely changing a word or two. In the short run, Bill could fool a stranger as to the real extent of his retardation.

One incident shows this: After Barry Morrow had moved on from the School of Social Work to the Department of Family Practice in the medical school (in 1978), he made a training tape using Bill as the subject. The idea was to teach the medical residents about the difficulties of communicating with special-needs patients. Anyway, Bill was filmed undergoing a fairly routine medical exam. The doctor, the chief medical resident, was obviously concerned about Bill's weight and eating habits. She advised Bill to eat lots of vegetables, refrain from alcohol, and stay away from starchy foods and red meat. She carefully inquired of Bill whether he fully understood the fairly simple instructions she had given him. He replied confidently, "No problem, doctor." So she sent some written instructions home with him.

About twenty-four hours later, Barry made a follow-up call to Bill to ask what recommendations the doctor had given him. Bill's reply, which would later bring down the house when shown to the residents in training, was, "She tol me to drink at least one beer a day and eats lots of meat and potato chips, buddy." Like others less mentally challenged, Bill had also managed to learn the technique of selective hearing.

The Early Childhood Education Center closed down about the third year of Bill's tenure at the coffee shop. Bill was heartbroken. He had always looked forward to greeting the children and paying a morning visit to their classroom. In fact, these activities had served as the highlights of his workday. With the children gone, Bill felt an emptiness.

However, as time went by, some of the social work students began to drop off their children at the coffee shop for Bill to babysit while they attended class.

One time, a secretary had received permission to bring her infant to work. Bill would spend hours helping to care for her child while she scurried to keep up with her work.

Bill's judgment might not always have been the best as a sitter, but his tenderness with children was phenomenal. As Barry and Bev had discovered early on, Bill could be trusted with children. While Bill might at times get bored and impatient, he would never become angry or violent. To Bill, children were innocent and helpless and needed the safety of trusting and caring adults.

I recall when one of the students asked Bill on several occasions to sit with her child while she was in class. This child was a redheaded girl, probably about nine years of age. One day, the girl came into my office, asking if I had seen Bill. She was worried because she thought Bill was lost, and he was supposed to be babysitting her. I suppressed a smile and joined her in searching for Bill. As we passed Professor Anders's office, I smelled cigar smoke. I knocked at the door, which after some hesitation, slowly opened. There sat our missing person with a big stogie in his mouth. Professor Anders explained that he was trying to clear up some misconceptions Bill had about Einstein's theory of relativity.

When Bill's workday ended around 4:30 P.M., he would amble over to the bus stop. Bill did not actually walk; he trudged somewhat stoop-shouldered and with eyes apparently focused on the ground. Despite the downward angle of his head when he walked, he rarely missed saying hello to a passing person. Or if he were being given a ride home, Bill would let his eyes roam the street corners and passing cars for people to wave to. Bill had an ability to read the eyes of strangers, knowing if and when it was proper to wave. Bill avoided those who might feel an intrusion, by keeping his eyes fixed to the ground.

Bill usually made his return trip to his Yewell Street boardinghouse by bus. The trip home was typically full of animated conversation, usually instigated by Bill. The regulars on the 4:30 P.M. bus were all looked upon by Bill as his friends. The driver, who was attuned to Bill's limitations, would let him know when it was time to get off. At his bus stop, Bill would thump down the stairs of the bus like an old turkey buzzard making an unexpected landing. He would look around for any neighbor friends with whom he could share the events of the day. Only if he found no one to talk to would he then head toward home.

I use-ta get up early to get to Norse Hall fore the childern arrived. I liked greetin' the childern and shakin' their hands. They would run up to me and shouts, "How are you, Bill?" And I'd tell 'em that God's given 'em a great day and how proud He was with how they looks. When they come to me, I take 'em by the hand and walk 'em to the door, then go back to get the next little one. Sometimes I could'n keep up, if they all started a comin' at once.

When all the childern were dropped off, I go and makes coffee. Barrymor had taught me how to make the coffee, but sometimes I get confuse. I'd have to throw the coffees away and makes some more. After the coffee's made, I takes a cup to Tom. I sits with Tom and talks a while till he asks me if I should'n be coverin' the coffee shops. Wished I could've spent more time talkin' to ol Tom, but he was real busy mos of the time.

I'd go back to the coffee shops, but if there was'n any peoples there, I'd go to see the childern. They was always happy to see me, but the teachers would sometimes get mad. One time, the head teacher got mad bout me showin' up in my Santa Claus suit. She tol Tom that I could'n visit her school if I was dressed up as Santas. It was against her religion or somethin'. Mos of the time, we would all go upstairs, so I could play my mouf organ for the childern. Then the teachers would read us stories. I liked listenin' to the stories. They'd be bout childern and animals and grown-ups.

At the school, they was always havin' meetin's. When they had a meetin', I would bring them coffees. Sometimes they'd be arguin' with each others, and to put it out of my mind, I would play my mouf organ. When I plays a polka, my spirits feel good and I can't think bout bad times or things. After a few songs, I'd listen again, and the meetin' seemed more friendly. The preacher in the isstitution use-ta say that makin' music is God singin' and God's singin' always makes people happy. That's why he'd let me play nearly ever'time he had services.

It was fun goin' home on the bus after work. All the peoples on the bus were my frens. Ever'buddy be laughin' and jokin' and askin' me to play the mouf organ. When the bus driver lets me off, ever'buddy on that bus would holler, "Bye, Bill, have a good nights." I'd tell 'em, "See you in the mornin's.

Don't let the bed bugs bite." I'd have to watch my steps gettin' off the buses, since my walkin' was'n so good after I had my bad leg.

It was the good times in Iowa Citys. I was jus glad to be out-a the isstitution. Jus' think, I have my own coffee shops and lotsa frens. What more could a person ask for? I jus thank God for all this happinesses.

9

Coming of Age

It is hard to know whether there was any real turning point in Bill's life in Iowa City that might have presaged his future celebrity. Bill simply followed a routine of working in the coffee shop on weekdays and dividing his weekends between helping Rosalie Rose in the shopping mall on Saturdays and helping me with refinishing projects on Sundays. In addition, he regularly attended Jewish, Catholic, and Protestant services on the weekends. Bill's evenings, of course, were filled with invitations from single mothers looking for a surrogate grandfather for their children and lonely students wanting a companion for a midweek movie.

What all this activity added up to was a great deal of personal visibility for Bill, most of which was quite positive. Bill was en route to becoming a noteworthy town figure. If there is a single early event that served to advance Bill's fame, it has to have been his Bar Mitzvah.

After Bill began routinely attending Jewish services, he gained the attention of Rabbi Portman, who found him a wonderful addition to the rather sparsely attended services at the synagogue. The rabbi suggested that perhaps Bill would like to have his Bar Mitzvah, even though by this time, Bill was nearly sixty-seven years of age. Bill, though vaguely aware of the meaning of the Bar Mitzvah, was nonetheless ready to say yes to anything associated with religion. So on July 7, 1979, Bill Sackter was initiated into Jewish manhood, with a large flock of well-wishers in attendance. Ironically, the majority of those in attendance were his friends from the Catholic and Protestant churches where he also regularly attended.

Did you knows I had a Bar Mitzvahs at the synagogue not many years ago? The rabbi asked me if I'd like a Bar Mitzvah, and I tol him I'd like that very much. I'd heard bout Bar Mitzvahs at home, and even once when I was in the isstitutions, one Jewish boy in my cottage went to St. Paul to have a Bar Mitzvah. The rabbi tol me the Bar Mitzvah is a way to show when you are a Jewish man and outgrowed being a boy. I was not jus a man, but an ol man when I got mine. Maybe cause I was crack-minded, it took me a little longer to grow than mos people.

The rabbi says to get a Bar Mitzvah, you have to be able to read the Torah and speak Hebrew. I tol him I probably could'n learn to reads the Hebrew, but I could speak it. Sometimes, I spoke it at synagogue already. So once't a week, the rabbi would have classes to teach me to speak Hebrew. It was pretty easy. All I had to do was listen to the sounds, and I could say the words. The rabbi would smiles when I speak Hebrew, but he must-a known what I was sayin' cause he would talk back to me in Hebrew. It was jus like Tom and me speakin' Swedish.

When the time came for my Bar Mitzvah, it was beautiful. Ever'thin was beautiful, with flowers and good smells. Mos of all, I was happy cause there was lotsa frens there, some even from Minnesotas. After the service, we had a big party right there in the social room of the synagogue. Jack brought some musicians with him from Minnesota, and I gots to play my mouf organ. Ever'buddy greeted me and says, "Good goin', Bill."

After that, I felt pretty good bout myselfs. I knew I was a Jewish man and had learned to speak Jewish. The peoples in the synagogue would come up and speak to me. They'd tell me, Bill, it is nice havin' me in our synagogue.

Tom wants me to talk bout other things that was important to me in Iowa Citys before they made the movies bout Mickey Roomies. Well, I liked givin' kids balloons to play with at the mall. Rosy invited me to go with her on Saturdays to helps her sell balloons. She'd get me all dressed up, like a clowns, and then have me hand out little balloons to the childern. I saw many of the kids from the Early Chilehood Center, 'n I met lotsa older childern. They'd come up and say, "Hi, Bill." Then they asks me to play my mouf organ.

The only problems with my job at the mall was my legs would get tired. I had a bad leg 'n a sore that won't heal. So I'd ask Rosy if I could'n sit on the benches for a while. She said that was fine. But I could see she wanted me workin' harder, so she could sell more balloons. I learned bout being a clown from my buddy, Jack.

I been pretty healthy. Far as I member, I never loss a day to my work cause of bein' sick. But one day, Barrymor caught me scratchin' my sore on my leg. He looked at it and turned white like a ghost. I tol him it ain't nothin', buddy, always been like that. But he made me go see ol Doc Caplan, who was some kind of specialist or somethin'. I don't like doctors much, but I knew Doc Caplan from the synagogue. He was a Jewish doctor. I liked that.

Well, when the doc saw my leg, he got mad. He says, "We got to put you in the hospital, Bill. Got to get that leg healed, or you're goin' loose it." Barrymor took me to the Oakdale Hospital. They were'n many peoples there, but I liked it. Many frens came. Barrymor came and snuck me a beer, and then Tom came and snuck me beer, too. I did'n say nothin' cause then I had two beers to drink. I got lotsa cards, too, the gets well kind-a cards. One came from my bus and was signed by all the passengers and the bus driver.

They cleaned my leg ever'day and put greasy stuff on it. Then Doc Caplan gave me a support sock for my leg and tol me I could go home. Only thing, I must keep my leg up at least half the time to get the circulations better. They had a nurse come 'n check it at home ever week after that for long as I can member.

As a reward for taking good care of his leg, I promised to take Bill to the state fair. Bill knew what state fairs were, but he had never been to one. So one mid-August day in 1976, Bill and I headed for Des Moines and the Iowa State Fair.

It was obvious Bill was looking forward to the visit. As we approached the fairgrounds, I could almost hear Bill's heart pounding. The parking lot was rather full, and I knew we would have a long walk to the entrance. We finally arrived, paid for our tickets, and began our tour of the attractions. It was apparent Bill had two main interests: eating as many goodies as he could afford and avoiding any scary rides. As for the latter concern, he did, however, try the merry-go-round and the bumper cars. He liked the bumper cars best. In fact, he used up almost all of his pocket money, twenty dollars, on this activity. This was, of course, after being assured that he did not have to buy food with his own money.

As Bill and I wandered about the fairgrounds, we chanced upon the beginning of a "Best Beard" contest that was being broadcast live by one of the local radio stations. Bill insisted on entering. "I gots the bes beard in this ol world," he said emphatically. There must have been about twelve competitors, most of whom looked pretty sophisticated. Well, as chance would have it, Bill was singled out as one of the top three finalists—all winners. Bill had come in third place in the audience voting.

Each of the three finalists were then interviewed by the host of the live radio program. The winner, a middle-aged botany professor from Iowa State University, was the first to be interviewed; the second-place finisher was a young salesman for Coca Cola Bottling Company, who worked out of Knoxville, Iowa. Both were asked a few personal questions, which they handled as if they were experienced at being interviewed live.

When it was Bill's turn, the young radio host asked, "Where do you work, Bill?" Bill replied, "I work at the universitys where I makes coffee for the peoples." A little taken aback, the announcer continued his questioning. "Which university do you work at?" Bill was puzzled by his question, having no idea that there was even more than one university in the entire world. He could only think to say, "At Iowas University." This troubled the radio host. What sort of interviewee did he have on his hands? So our host shifted direction and asked Bill how old he was. Bill replied, "Thirty-four," the age he had always given during most of his adult life. Numbers themselves registered no meaning with Bill.

The commentator knew Bill was much older than thirty-four, and he was becoming rather flustered by this talkative, but confused, old man. However, by the time the announcer was about to ask his next question, Bill had his harmonica in his mouth and was playing the "Too Fat Polka." Having lost most of his cool and his cockiness, the host was only too glad to wrap up his coverage of the Best Beard contest. He handed Bill his third-place prize and hurriedly ushered him off the stage. As Bill headed down the several steps to the general seating area, he looked up at the audience and waved as if he were some dignitary disembarking a plane to an awaiting crowd of well-wishers. This was the first of many awards that would come Bill's way.

One day in 1977, a student (whose name has since been forgotten), who was physically challenged, came to see me about nominating Bill for Iowa's Handicapped Citizen of the Year award. Interestingly enough, this was not a student from the School of Social Work, but a student from the College of Business.

I was enthusiastic about the idea, though not optimistic about Bill's chances. Normally, this was an award that would be won by some highly successful, physically handicapped person, such as a prosperous business-man or college professor in a wheelchair. I reflected on how much we had taken Bill for granted up to this point. We simply enjoyed his presence but would have never thought on our own to put him up for such a nomination. We knew Bill was special, but we had not thought much about how others might regard him.

With my help, the student filled out the application to nominate Bill. Next, we needed to write a narrative explaining what Bill had done to war-rant this nomination. With the student's permission, I asked Barry to write it. I figured Barry knew Bill much better than either of us.

To our knowledge, Barry really had not written much of anything at this point in his young career. Communication for him was through the me-dium of film, especially video, not the written word. Nonetheless, Barry took on the assignment and completed a brilliant 1500-word essay. The applica-tion packet was mailed off by the student, who had taken it upon himself to be Bill's advocate for this award.

Months passed, and the competition was forgotten, until the student returned one day to say that Bill had been selected as the Iowa Handicapped Citizen of the Year. Both Barry and I were astounded and elated. We really did not think Bill had had a chance. As I said, such awards usually go to successful businessmen in wheelchairs. We were informed the award would be given to Bill in November in conjunction with the Governor's Conference on Disabilities in Des Moines. Everyone at the School of Social Work, of course, was excited with the news, except perhaps for Bill, who really did not understand what the award was and what it meant.

When the time came for the Governor's Conference, I arranged to rent a large charter bus to accommodate the students and faculty who wanted to attend the awards ceremony and support Bill. On the trip to Des Moines, Bill's friends and colleagues chattered with excitement. They carried on like a bunch of teenagers going to a football game with some arch-rival.

There was much singing and fooling around on the bus trip, which predictably got Bill's motor running. Before long, he was on center stage in the middle of the bus, playing his harmonica and dancing. People clapped and stomped their feet in time to his rhythms.

The awards dinner and ceremony could not have gone better. All of Bill's supporters were seated together. When the time arrived to present the award, Governor Robert Ray asked Bill to come forward. He did, accompanied by his guardian at the time, Barry Morrow. The governor read the proclamation naming Bill Sackter as the Iowa Handicapped Citizen of the Year. Bill stepped forward to receive the award plaque and then, without hesitation, greeted the audience, sharing some of his usual lines: "Thank you very much, ladies and gentlemens. I am prouds for this award. I have had some bad times in my lifes, but these are the good times. God bless you all. God loves you. Thank you very much. Shalom."

Without premeditation, Bill pulled his Hohner harmonica from his pocket and played his favorite song. The sounds produced a foot-tapping from the audience that could be likened to a modified two-step dance. Then, with Barry's prompting, came a synchronized clapping. Bill was reluctant to stop. After all, this was a climax in his life. Barry managed to step on Bill's foot, as if it were a brake, and Bill slowed to his "shave and a haircut" ending. The audience jumped to their feet and cheered. The governor was delighted.

With a nudge from Barry, Bill reached into his pocket and brought out a shiny new harmonica as a gift to the governor. Diplomatically, Governor Ray struggled with a few notes on his unexpected present. The audience giggled, but with filled hearts. For all concerned, they might just as well have been at the Academy Awards.

I don't how it happens, but I got a gubenor's award for being crack-minded. I tried to splains it to Barry, but he tol me it was'n for bein' crack-minded, but cause I was ever'buddy's Bill. I guess they mus give wards for havin' lotsa frens or somethin'. Anyway, me and my frens got to go on a universitys bus to the Capitol to attend a dinner. The gubenor was there, and he gave me a ward. I forgot what it says. Mus be somethin' bout me runnin' a coffee shop. Then I gave the gubenor a mouf organ. Barrymor thought this'd be a good idea. The gubenor, he tried to plays it, but he don't know how. Maybe he'll meet somebuddy like ol Joe to teach him.

They had a good supper at this ward thing. I brought Mae, Angela, and Kenny to eats there, too, that way Mae did'n have to fix no supper. They even had my favorite food—chicken. Only problem was there was only one piece on each plate with some tatoes and vegetables. Truffully, it was'n enough to eat. I was hungry all the ways home. But I did'n mine being hungry cause it had been a nice party and I had the first ward I've ever gotten in my life, 'cept for the one at the state fair.

Tom and Barrymor tol me they was proud of ol Bill. All my frens says they was happy for me. You know, buddy, it jus does'n get any better'n this. I had the bad times, but no more. I ain't never goin' back to an isstitution. I'm goin' stay and live with Mae. I got a family now, and that's where I belongs.

The day after Bill's award, the *Des Moines Register* ran a special on Bill's story. It was, in fact, the narrative Barry had submitted for the Iowa Handicapped Citizen of the Year competition. The story included a large picture of Bill playing his harmonica at the awards ceremony and was prominently placed on the front page of the Today section. Barry's story would one day make it into the *Congressional Record*.

The *Register* column must have been widely read because letters from all over the state began to pour in. A secretary had to be assigned to help Bill handle his correspondence. One letter came from a man who owned the Mr. Executive Hair Stylist Salon in Des Moines. He offered to make Bill a wig that would perfectly match his distinguished gray beard. The offer was enthusiastically accepted by Bill and would result in a whole new appearance for him. The wig would become a metaphor for the new persona that Bill had taken on.

Before the excitement of Bill's award had settled, Barry was contacted by an official in Washington and notified that Bill had come in second place in a national competition for handicapped person of the year. None of us even knew that his materials had been submitted for that competition as well. Apparently, the U.S. senators of the top finalists were notified of their constituents' selection. It was through Senator Dick Clark's office that we were notified of Bill's national recognition.

It was Barry who received a call from Senator Clark, inviting Bill to come to Washington for a weekend as his guest. Barry consulted with me about the offer, and I agreed this was something that could not be passed up. Money would be found to support the trip. Arrangements were finally made

for Barry and Bill to head to Washington on the following Thursday afternoon. I would join them on Saturday. Bill was to be escorted to see the town
on Friday and Saturday morning by one of the senator's aides. Reservations
were made for the three of us at a modestly priced room in a downtown
Holiday Inn.

Bill was taken on the standard "cooks' tour" of Washington by one of
Senator Clark's aides. The itinerary included stops at Arlington National
Cemetery, where Bill insisted on kneeling on the concrete to pray for the
soldiers, and at the Lincoln Memorial, where Bill declared he was a free man
now, too. Barry tagged along as Bill's interpreter, though Bill's official guide
and Bill got along famously. I doubt whether this aide would ever again have
a tourist like Bill. Even though Bill was now well into his sixties, the pace of
the tour did not tire him. All this attention kept his adrenalin level sky high.

Bill's special tour included lunch in the Senate dining room on the
second day of his visit. His lunch mates, in addition to Barry and Senator
Clark, included Senators Edward Kennedy and Jacob Javits. This group of
senators were clearly the nucleus of Washington's liberal establishment at
the time. We don't know whether Bill had bean soup or not, but we do know
he managed to get his hands on a Senate cigar.

The luncheon of congressional dignitaries apparently taxed Bill's patience. Barry recognized this and suggested that Bill might want to stretch his
legs. He could easily walk the rotunda without fear of getting lost. Bill agreed
to restrict his explorations to the floor they were on. Excusing himself, he
left the table and began wandering a Senate hallway.

It should be noted that this was a somewhat exceptional week in Washington. There had been a diplomatic crisis over some international event. So
diplomats from all over the world had come scurrying to Washington, and
their presence in the Senate building would not have been surprising.

Bill was impeccably dressed in a new, three-piece, dark pinstripe suit.
He wore his new wig, which fully complemented his recently groomed beard.
With a cigar in his mouth, he certainly looked the part of a visiting dignitary.
Thus, we should not have been surprised when a certain well-known Southern senator stopped Bill in the hallway to say hello. Apparently, Bill had
caught the senator's eye, and they had exchanged greetings. Unknown to Bill
and the senator, Barry was watching from a short distance and had chosen to

film Bill's self-styled mini-tour with a small, handheld movie camera. Barry captured their exchange on film. The senator initially made some small talk to which Bill could respond without difficulty. This was followed by an inquiry about whether Bill was here for the special diplomatic hearing. The senator also asked Bill what country did he represent. Bill was confused by the questions, but as always, this never interfered with some sort of response. The gibberish that Bill uttered puzzled the senator for a moment. The senator it seems had decided that English must be Bill's second language, and that without an interpreter, further conversation at this level would be impossible. So the senator smiled, Bill responded, and the two shook hands and exchanged their good-byes.

For those who have seen the movie *Being There* with Peter Sellers, it was apparent that, while Bill probably could not have been taken seriously as a presidential candidate, he easily could have posed as a foreign diplomat with limited English abilities. In a way, English really was Bill's second language. Speaking his own unique tongue was in fact his first language.

Clark's office had arranged for Bill to meet President Jimmy Carter on Saturday in the Oval Office of the White House. The diplomatic crisis, however, had altered the plans. Instead, Mrs. Carter was there to meet Bill.

When he met the First Lady, Bill was awestruck by her appearance. His first words, even before an exchange of hellos took place, were, "You sure are pretty." Bill then managed a bit of small talk before asking Mrs. Carter if her daughter Amy was around. He said he would really like to meet her since he was so fond of children. Bill wanted to know where she was, what she was doing, and whether he could play the harmonica for her. Unfortunately, she was in school. Bill was given a picture of the Carter family as a goodwill gesture.

By Saturday evening, Barry was tired of chaperoning Bill. Bill, on the other hand, seemed little worse for the wear. By this point, Barry's adrenalin level had been running on high for nearly three days, plus he had some friends in Washington he wanted to see. Thus when I arrived, Bill was immediately turned over to my gentle care for the evening. The official tour was by then over, and we were on our own. I told Barry that I would be happy to take over as Bill's companion and that we would find some way to entertain ourselves on a Saturday night in the nation's capital.

My reunion with Barry and Bill took place in the hotel room just about cocktail hour. Barry had brought a bottle of spirits with him, and soon the three of us were engaged in a toast or two or three (maybe even four) to Bill's good fortune. By the time Barry left for the evening, both Bill and I were testing the limits of sobriety. I felt it was time for us to find some supper and sponge up some of the alcoholic content in our blood. Less steadily than I would have wished, we exited our hotel.

Once we were on the sidewalk, it became apparent that we were not in one of the better parts of the downtown area. Our hotel was located on one of the more active "solicitation" corners of the city. Prostitutes were as common as bureaucrats. Bill, naturally, had a smile and a greeting for each and every lady of the night. He assumed their interest in us was just plain Washington friendliness.

Finding food turned out to be more complicated than I had planned. Our first attempt at finding an inexpensive meal landed us at a nearby tavern, which served only liquor. Since we were already seated and the waiter had approached, we ordered a beer in order to avoid the embarrassment of just getting up and leaving.

This was not good, especially when we made the same mistake a block later. Two beers on top of an afternoon of brandy were not making us any more sober. Nearly an hour had passed since Bill and I had left our hotel in pursuit of our evening repast. Then, at last, we stumbled into one of those franchise buffeterias. Bill was elated with the endless varieties of food items to choose from. He took his tray and immediately covered it with everything in sight, including at least two entrees. I filled my own tray separately and followed him to the cash register where I picked up the tab.

Bill successfully negotiated his amply filled tray in the direction of an unoccupied table. I followed. On arrival, he cautiously lowered his tray and managed to miss the table by a full two feet. The tray and its contents exploded on the floor. Busboys rushed to the rescue. Bill remained unruffled.

With no embarrassment, I nudged Bill forward the final two feet and sat him down at the table. Setting my own tray in front of him, I ordered him to eat while I returned a second time for my own food. We ate in silence, waiting for the meal to help sober us up, while all the world continued to stare in our direction. We were undoubtedly the oddest couple at dinner.

Fortunately, Bill and I were dressed well enough that they could not write us off as a couple of homeless winos.

I had assumed Bill must be feeling as I did, slightly nauseous and anxious. I was not really having a good time. My choice would have been to return to the hotel and spend Saturday night in front of the television set. Bill, however, would have none of it. He was ready to party. Washington was his town, or at least, it had been his for a few days. His moment of embarrassment at having dropped his tray had disappeared. The food had fueled his energy and had given him back his steady step. He looked at me, and asked, "Where to now, buddy?"

I had a good supper that nights with Tom, although truffully, I did have an accident. I was carryin' my trays to the table. It was full of the bes food I'd never seen. My legs was not too good. You know, buddy, I got one real bad leg where the aides kicked me when I was in isstitution. For some reasons, my eyes was'n too good that night, either. Too many beers. I put my tray down, but there was'n no table under it. Oo-ee, it made a mess when it crashed to the floor.

Tom, he gave me his food and went back to get more for hisself. I could see he was mad at me. So we did'n say nothin' durin' our eatin'. After I finished though, I was feelin' pretty good. I wanted to see ol Washington. I tol Tom we should go lookin' round. He was'n too happy with my suggestion, but he followed me jus the same.

First things I know, I finds more of those pretty ladies who was so interested in me and Tom. They followed us into a park, where I wanted to rest a minute and talk with my frens. A couple of the ladies followed us and sat next to us. I figured they wanted me to play 'em a song. So I bring out my mouf organ and plays. They starts clappin', one even does some dancin', and first things we know, there is a whole bunch of peoples round us. Some was askin' for quarters, which I give 'em, and others was givin' me quarters for playin'. It was really somethin'.

Fore we lef, there must-a been a hundert peoples round us, dancin' and tappin' their feets. Tom seemed to get nervous and tried to talk me into leavin', but I did'n wanna go cause they were such nice frens.

The ladies followed us back to our hotels, but Tom tells them it was my bedtime. They laughs and said that's what it's all bout, ol man.

It was okay. I was gettin' tired, and I had had a good time, anyway.

Tom tol me to forget bout takin' a shower, jus get into bed. Next thing I knew, we was all sleepin' together—me, Barrymor, and Tom.

The next day, we had to go back to Iowa Citys. Never will I ever forgets that trip. Met lotsa nice people, even Mrs. Carter. Did'n get to see Amy, though. She was in school. But I saw statues and graveyards, ate lotsa good food, and had me a couple of beers, too. Shalom, ol Washington.

10

Fame Finds Bill

Bill had taken one step toward celebrity status with his Handicapped Citizen of the Year award. He seemed to wear the attention well, fully enjoying his experiences. In the process, he cultivated many friendships. In some of our post-Washington discussions about Bill, Barry and I came to an agreement that Bill's story deserved to be more widely shared. There were so few examples of a man with Bill's limitations having had such a powerful impact on so many people.

As director of the School of Social Work, I had become increasingly aware of Barry's creativity as a filmmaker. Thus, it seemed completely natural to encourage Barry to work on a documentary about Bill's life. If Barry would try his hand at a media statement, I would try to locate some funding for such a project.

In the coming weeks, I authored grants to the Kennedy Foundation in Washington, D.C., and to the Northwest Area Foundation in Minneapolis. Both seemed highly appropriate potential supporters. The Kennedy Foundation focused exclusively on the mentally handicapped, and the Northwest Area Foundation had a special grants program for funding young filmmakers.

Unfortunately, neither foundation was interested, and another year of wishing and waiting would pass. In the interim, however, Barry had produced a multimedia synopsis of Bill's story that was very moving. It was shown to a number of potential funders, who reacted favorably to the presentation. Nevertheless, they all failed to produce any tangible offers of support. Finally, nearly two years after work on the multimedia presentation had been completed, an invitation to present it to the Board of Directors of the University of Iowa Foundation was received. Our dog-and-pony show was to be presented to the board at the conclusion of its September 1980 board meeting.

As the last agenda item on the board's slate, Barry showed his media project, and I spoke to its importance and our shared dream of making a full-fledged documentary of Bill's story. By the conclusion of our pitch, I had thought the board to be attentive and appreciative. However, no specific discussion ensued about what role, if any, the board would or could play in getting a documentary made. What did happen, though, was that one board member sequestered Barry and asked him if he would be willing to make a presentation to a group in New York City the following week. This board member turned out to be a vice president of Mobil Oil stationed in their East Coast offices.

An excited Barry Morrow assured him that he would be honored to attend the New York City meeting. Barry, working day and night, put some final touches on his product and headed to New York the following week. Barry assumed he would be meeting some Mobil Oil corporate types associated with their foundation. When he arrived at the meeting, however, he found himself facing a group of CBS network television officials.

When the meeting with the TV moguls ended, Barry called me on the telephone. "Tom," he said with his voice dropping. "They don't want to fund a documentary." I felt heavy again. Yet another rejection.

Then Barry's voice literally leapt out, as he yelled, "But they want to do a television movie about Bill's life!" I was trying to push through Barry's excitement, wanting to know who they was.

"CBS television, network television, buddy, and they want me to help work on the screen treatment," Barry replied.

This seemed a little larger than life to both Barry and I. Our interest in sharing Bill with a broader public had never, ever included the prospect of a movie.

Like a secluded monk, Barry spent the next month and a half shut away in an office in the basement of Oakdale Hall, part of the University of Iowa campus that had once been a hospital for tuberculosis patients. When he emerged, he had completed a ninety-page manuscript about Bill's life, a so-called screen treatment. It was immediately express-mailed to the CBS people. Several months later, Barry was notified that it had passed through stage one of the moviemaking process. Barry was asked if he would be interested in participating in stage two, the writing of the actual screenplay. He accepted the offer and was unknowingly on his way to a future Hollywood career as a writer, producer, and director.

As a writer without a publication record, Barry was retained for a minimum fee. He was joined by another professional writer, who would soon be dispatched to the School of Social Work to spend ten days in Wild Bill's Coffeeshop getting to know Bill and his routine.

Months later, Barry and the professional writer, Corey Blechman, completed the screenplay. This, too, passed the rigorous review of the CBS film editors.

The time had finally arrived to cast the film, find a director, and push for a December 1981 airing. The television programming people believed Bill's story was natural for a Christmas season showing.

The casting process was open to speculation. Ed Asner was the hands-on choice to play the role of Bill, but he could not rearrange his schedule. The distant second choice was Mickey Rooney, whose career had been on hold for nearly a decade, and who no longer had instant audience appeal, especially with the younger generations. In addition, Mr. Rooney was under a year's contract to star in the musical *Sugar Babies*. Rooney was eventually chosen for the part, despite the problem of having to film around his performances of *Sugar Babies*.

In addition to Rooney, a rising star by the name of Dennis Quaid was chosen to play the role of Bill's guardian (Barry). A young Helen Hunt was selected to play Barry's wife, Bev. The director was Anthony Page, who had recently directed the film, *I Never Promised You a Rose Garden*.

Owing to Rooney's *Sugar Babies* performance schedule, the University of Iowa setting was shot at a small, private college in Yonkers, New York. Yonkers afforded a good location for some winter scenes, which called for "Minnesota" snow. Other scenes and some of the movie's finales were filmed in Dallas, Texas, where Rooney had an extended engagement with *Sugar Babies*.

It would be on the set in Dallas that Rooney would finally meet the man whom he had been portraying. Mickey invited Bill to spend some time on the set during the filming. During his weekend in Dallas, Bill was also invited to a performance of *Sugar Babies*. At the end of his Saturday night *Sugar Babies* performance, Mickey invited Bill on stage. Mickey introduced Bill to his audience and then presented him with a big, ten-gallon hat with Bill's name on it.

Interpreting Bill's character would have been a mean feat for any actor, including the very talented Mickey Rooney. Rooney had insisted that he had to interpret the story's character without attempting to study the Bill persona. His first characterization was so overdrawn, however, that Barry was forced to remind the producers of the contract they had signed to get Bill's rights. The contract stated that in no way could the movie present Bill in ways that would belittle or denigrate him. Bill was not to be presented as some sort of imbecile, no matter how charming the portrayal.

Mickey reluctantly accepted the criticism and returned with a much-improved improvisation of Bill. To those who knew Bill, even the improved characterization bore little resemblance to Bill, but it did present a person to whom audiences were positively drawn. After all, Bill's story was not a documentary but a docudrama—a more or less fictionalized biography.

In early December 1981, the film was ready, and a premiere of the movie was arranged in Iowa City. The University of Iowa Foundation, the same organization that had been instrumental in the movie's development, arranged for a town-and-gown showing in Hancher Auditorium, the University of Iowa's performing arts center.

Planning for the premiere went on with a great fury. Bill and Barry were to arrive in a black limousine just before the showing, accompanied by a CBS vice president. I was to give a welcome and share some background about the movie's history. Then the film would be shown. Afterwards, Barry and Bill would come on stage for bows and questions. The CBS vice president would share a few words, and the entire community would be invited over to the School of Social Work for a reception. The reception was to be organized by the women of Agudas Achim Synagogue.

The event could not have been more successful. Along with the showing of the film, Bill and Barry's onstage appearance was a hit. Bill's animated presence, his thoroughly authentic words, and his harmonica playing made the premiere a night to remember. The reception was jammed with well-wishers and had all the earmarks of an event that might never end. When it did end, however, sometime after midnight, Bill was whisked by limousine back to his boardinghouse at 1311 Yewell Street.

Bill returned to work the very next morning at his regular time. He was back to being Bill. For him, nothing had essentially changed in his life. He had children to greet, coffee to make, and smiles to bring to people's faces.

Becoming a national figure, a minor celebrity of sorts, had obviously not been one of Bill's life goals. That it actually happened was far more important to the rest of us than to Bill. He never really grasped what it meant to have a hundred million people view the story of his life. He loved the moments of attention but never really associated them with anything he had somehow earned. If anything, he thought maybe people just liked his harmonica playing.

Bill would have many more occasions to be on stage, but from his perspective, he had been there before. Hadn't he done the gigs with Barry and his band? Hadn't he won third place in the Iowa State Fair beard contest? Hadn't he appeared before several thousand people at the movie's premiere? Weren't all the new invitations really just the result of having lots of friends?

Bill's reaction to all the hoopla that went with public attention may best be evidenced in his reaction to the movie the night it was shown on national television. Bill and I had been invited to the home of social work professor Wayne Johnson for supper and to watch the television airing of the film. Wayne was the senior member of the social work faculty and a long-time fan and supporter of Bill.

Most of those gathered seemed to have their eyes glued on Bill rather than on the television production. Everyone was curious as to how Bill would react to seeing himself portrayed on television. Midway into the story, however, Professor Johnson poked me and pointed toward Bill. He had fallen asleep. I immediately nudged Bill back to consciousness. Noting his faux pas, Bill aimed his attention toward the TV and tried to feign interest in the remainder of the program.

Bill had always thought it his duty to assure others he was having a good time. The truth was he could care less about the movie of his life. The fun for him was over once the good food was gone. True to form, Bill drifted back to sleep again. This time, no one bothered to wake him.

As the last commercial ran for the *CBS Sunday Night Movie*, the phone began to ring off the hook. There had been some prearranged, post-film interviews with reporters that I was to handle for Bill, since Barry had been called away to attend a more formal gathering in California.

The first call went something like this:

"Is Bill Sackter there? I am the movie critic for the *New York Times*."

"Yes, this is ol Bill. How you do?"

"What did you think of the movie and the way Mickey Rooney portrayed your life?"

"Let me tell you, buddy, ol Mickey Roomies is a regular good guy. He loves childern, and they follows him round. He went to the hospital to see the little girl. He even works in a coffee shop jus like me. Me and Mickey Roomies life is lots alike."

"What do you think will happen to your life now that you are, one may say, famous?"

"Well, to tell the trufs, I got lotsa work to do in the coffee shops. And Mae says I gotta clean my room. She says God loves those that keep their rooms clean."

"Do you have anything special you would like to tell our viewers?"

"You jus tell 'em ol Bill's got a good life now. He had troubles years ago, but things is goin' good. He is gettin' to be a regular, good man, not a crack-minded ol' man. God loves ever'buddy, shalom."

"Thank you, Bill."

I think I ate too much chickens for supper, cause I sure got sleepy in the movie. I know I fell asleep cause Tom poked me to wake up. Anyhow, I knew mos of the story bout Mickey Roomie's life anyways. He 'vited me down to Texas to visit him not long ago. He tol me what he was doin'. I tol him his life was sure a lot like my lifes. I unnerstan how he feels. When the movie was over, I felt pretty rested. Lotsa peoples called me and asked me questions bout the movie. I joyed talkin' to 'em, but after while, it got to be borin', so Tom talked to 'em for me. Tom's a good fren.

The movie, as history would record, was a hit. The initial viewership numbered nearly forty million. Eventually, well over a hundred million people would see the movie, not counting the equal number of overseas viewers who would see it in movie theaters. The critics' response to the film was unexpectedly positive. CBS had premonitions that the film had the potential to go big with a mass audience, yet network officials realized this was their first attempt in this genre—a feature film about a mentally challenged person.

The film was included in the screen critics' competition known as the Golden Globe Awards. Like the Emmy Awards ceremony, the Golden Globe ceremony was nationally televised. With Bill and company as nominees, a number of invitations were extended to those involved in the making of the film. Not only was Barry invited to attend, but so was Bill. Mickey Rooney had asked him to receive the Best Actor award on his behalf should he be selected.

In their rented Hollywood tuxedos, Bill and Barry attended one of the premier extravaganzas of the television season—the Golden Globe Awards ceremony—held in January 1982.

Most of Bill's friends, definitely those of us who were with him and Barry daily in the School of Social Work, were watching the night of the awards ceremony. When the best actor category was finally announced, we could hardly believe our ears. Mickey Rooney came away with top honors for his portrayal of our Bill.

We had debated often the merits of Mickey's performance and agreed he was no Bill. Yet we accepted the fact that he had successfully given the viewers a positive and sympathetic portrayal of a person challenged by mental deficiency. He made the social intent of the film work from our point of view, namely, to inform viewers that mentally challenged persons need not be feared and that most are contributing members of society.

Rooney's selection meant that Bill and Barry would have to climb to the stage, face forty million people, and Bill would have to say some words of appreciation on Mickey Rooney's behalf. The cameras followed them from their first startled look at hearing Rooney's name called to their march to the podium. It was Barry who first reacted to hearing Rooney's name announced as Best Actor. Bill simply mimicked Barry's response. For Bill, if the world was clapping he should be clapping. If people acted surprised, he would try his best to also act surprised. I am sure Bill had not fully comprehended the significance of the moment. Whatever the occasion, however, he was out to make it a good time.

Although Barry had previously instructed Bill on what they should do if Mickey won, Bill had long since forgotten. With no time for a crash review, Barry simply took Bill by the arm and led him to the podium. There was no predicting how Bill would actually handle the tension of the moment. Barry had attempted to rehearse Bill about what would be expected of him. Yet Barry knew from the past that Bill would nod his head in agreement with any offered guidance and then do what he darned pleased.

Part of Barry's rehearsal had been quite painful. At the insistence of the CBS vice president for television specials (who had attended the Iowa City premiere), Barry was told to literally strip Bill of his harmonica. There was to be no goofball "Too Fat Polka" aired on national television. Barry hated himself for doing it. Not only did he tell Bill about the rules being imposed, he demanded that Bill turn over his harmonica to him. Bill, with great reluctance and no small degree of protest, finally did so.

The master of ceremonies introduced Bill by announcing, "On behalf of Mickey Rooney, who could not be present, his award will be accepted by Bill Sackter, whose life it was that was depicted in the film, *Bill*."

Without hesitation and with total self-confidence, Bill began his reply: "Thank you, ladies and gentlemens for 'vitin' me. I wanna accept this ward for my fren Mickey Roomies. He is a good man, and he had a good life. I gonna give him this ward. God loves you all, thank you very much. Shalom."

As Barry was reaching for Bill's arm to lead him off the stage, Bill reached into his coat pocket, pulled out a backup harmonica, grabbed for the mike, and started playing his rendition of the "Too Fat Polka." Barry was devastated, and the CBS vice president, mortified. Bill played on. Within seconds, however, Jane Fonda, seated at one of the tables closest to the stage, got in rhythm with Bill's tapping foot and started clapping in harmony with Bill's tune. Soon the entire Golden Globe audience was doing the same. Finally, with no little prompting from Barry, Bill ended his impromptu performance to a standing ovation. An authentic touch of humanity had penetrated what otherwise had been a slick, predictable television extravaganza.

At the conclusion of the program, Barry was plotting a quick escape with Bill to avoid a major chewing out by the producer of the awards program. He knew that artistic temperaments would not stand for a retarded man stealing the show, especially when he and Bill had been warned to keep the program free from any embarrassment Bill might inadvertently cause. Before they made it to the winners' press conference, though, Barry and Bill were wrapped in the arms of the producer. He spoke to them as one, "You guys were just great. You added the touch the program was missing. I am forever grateful. Bill, you are some kind of guy."

Hey Barrymor, that was lotsa fun at the wards ceremony. You got a bowlin' trophy, and so did Mickey Roomie. Ever'buddy looked so nice. You looks pretty good, too, buddy. I am sure glad I membered to bring another mouf organ cause I knew those frens would want to hear me play. Did I do okay, buddy? Maybe we can do that again next years. I likes comin' to Californias.

I really joyed meetin' your sister. (Barry's sister Cloyce was, at the time, a well-known television and film actress.) She's got herself a nice place with swimmin' pools and ever'thin. Hope we can go there again. She's got good cold beers, and I got to soak my legs in her pool.

Where we goin' stay tonight, Barrymor? Don't forget, I gotta get back to Iowa as soon as possible or nobuddy's goin' to have any coffees.

The few short years that followed Bill's introduction to celebrity prominence were something to behold. Letters started to pour in from all over the country. Bill received as many as eight to ten letters and cards a day. The spread of interest and response was incredible. There were, of course, many letters and drawings sent him by children. In one way or another, each would say thank you to Bill for being such a nice man. A second group of fans were adults who had had troubled pasts or were locked away in institutions. The most common of these respondents were prisoners. Some wrote simply to say how much they enjoyed the movie; others shared a hope that they might also escape from infamy and neglect as Bill had. A few, along with the children, wondered if they couldn't begin a pen pal relationship with Bill. No one asked for money, fortunately, because Bill had none, either before or after the movie.

The voluminous correspondence required some additional secretarial assistance, which the school willingly provided. Bill needed help to both read the contents of these correspondences and to draft replies. None went unanswered. The school was a bit overwhelmed by this fortuitous happening and was somewhat unprepared for how to deal with much of it.

The many letters and cards Bill received were soon followed by invitations to attend various conferences and programs. These invitations came from a variety of organizations. Many of the groups wanted to present awards of one kind or another to Barry, Bill, or both. The range of these invitations could not have been broader. The most interesting invitation came from the American Academy for Cerebral Palsy and Developmental Medicine, which invited Bill to their annual meeting. The most frequent invitations came from state chapters or programs connected with retarded citizens, followed by invitations from colleges and universities.

In all, Bill would go on to receive dozens more awards. Following his death in 1983, a national award would be named after him by the Association of Retarded Citizens (the Arc). The Bill Sackter Award is given annually to the mentally challenged adult who has made a major contribution to the well-being of others and to his/her community.

Beyond these many invitations, there were some special recognitions that merit elaboration. One such recognition was conferred during a week-long visit to Arizona, arranged by the Arizona Association of Retarded Citizens. One activity on Bill's itinerary was a visit to the Arizona State Legislature. There, the Arizona speaker rose to read the following proclamation:

> We, the membership of the Thirty-Sixth Legislature, in the State of Arizona, gather today in tribute to you, Bill Sackter. You live in a world filled with surprise and chaos, yet you have the unique ability to filter out the harsh ideas, pain, and sorrow and accept your life for the beautiful thing it really is. What we see in the distance as

problems looking like despair, you see a rainbow of hope. To us, a returned smile is not enough, to you, it is all that really matters. Those things that nature took away, God has made up for in the myriad of magic in your perception of life. We know your spontaneous affection for each of us has no ulterior motivation. That fact, in itself, endears you to our hearts more than you could ever know. For allowing us inside and helping us to appreciate the feelings of those with mental retardation and for allowing us and bearing with us while we mature to meet your clarity of emotion, we stand in salute to you, Bill Sackter. May God bless your every step.
—Stan Turley, President

One would not have expected such a perceptive and poetic statement to come from a busy legislative body. Bill's honorary state citizenship recognition was only the second time in that state's history that such recognition had ever been extended to a non-Arizonan.

Bill's invitation to be the halftime guest of the new Phoenix Wrangler professional football team was just as unexpected. A crowd of nearly fifty thousand were in attendance to watch its newly franchised team the evening Bill was honored. With the score favoring the home team at the end of the second quarter, the halftime program began.

The event had all the elements necessary to get Bill's engine revved. There were fireworks, followed by the cheerleader corps dancing and, later, a loud and brassy rock music group. Then with spotlights focused on the fifty yard line, Bill was trotted out with Barry to be introduced to the crowd. The master of ceremonies presented Bill with a football sweatshirt with his name and the number 00 on it, along with a plaque identifying him as a honorary member of Phoenix football team. The MC then read to Bill and the crowd a congratulatory letter from President Reagan.

Bill, who was surprisingly athletic, was then invited to throw the football to his buddy, Barry. And, of course, with a microphone in front of him, Bill could not leave without giving the Sunday night football crowd a sample of his harmonica playing.

By this time, Bill was getting the hang of showmanship. He had always done by instinct the right things to capture the sentiments of a crowd. Only at this point, he started doing those things with a little more flare. His confidence kept growing and growing but never beyond a certain level of humility, which separated him from many others who had acquired celebrity status. For Bill, these events were all just parties, full of fun, friends, and food—the three basic ingredients he cared about.

It sure was somethin', goin' out onto the fields at have-times. I never knew bout the Stranglers fore I come to Arizona. I never seen such big peoples in my life. We had one fellow whose name was Monster in the isstitutions. He must-a been a footballs player cause he was bout same size as a Strangler. When Monster died, they had to build a special coffins to bury him in. His coffin was twice as big as a regular one.

Bes thing of all was seein' them fireworks and listenin' to the good musics. I wished I could have danced with the cheerleader girls cause the music was makin' my feet move so much. But they did 'vites me to the middle of the field, and I played 'em a song on my mouf organ. Then they gave me a big footballs shirt with my name on it. When I got back to Iowas, I gave the football shirts to Tom. He hung it up in the coffee shop next to the cowboy hat Mickey Roomie gave me.

We had good times with the frens in Arizona. They works with folks like me. They took me and Barrymor to see lots of retarded peoples, where they work and lives. I feel sorry for retarded peoples, specially if their mamas and dads put them in isstitutions. Isstitutions ain't no good for nobuddy. It brought me the hard times in my life. But you can see, I got the good times now.

When Barrymor and me had to talk in front of the groups, we would fool around a little. Barrymor, he'd tease me and would say things that would make ever'buddy laugh. We'd keep it up for a long time. Then peoples would start askin' us questions. I'd answer the questions, but Barrymor would helps me out.

We went back to Iowa cause I needed to get back to work, buddy. Gettin' to see places round was somethin' I joyed, but I had my work to do. If you're goin' to be a regular good man, you gots to work. Mae, Kenny, and Angela all was pretty sad when I was'n home. So I was glad to be back, I'll tell you that.

11
The Man Who Would Be Santa

In these reflections on Bill's celebrity—a celebrity that would be cut short by his untimely death—one cannot help but think what an unlikely candidate he had been to brush shoulders with fame and fortune. He had spent forty-four of his precious years in an institution for the feeble-minded, having passed through its gates at the tender age of seven. Bill's age exceeded his IQ when he was finally discharged back to the community after nearly a half century of incarceration.

Yet, a flash of fame did come his way, though admittedly fortune eluded him. He would die as he had always lived, a certified pauper. What on earth had he done to draw the kind of attention he did, if only for a few fleeting years?

Bill clearly had a special charm that drew people of all ages, races, and social classes. His inner self flowed with such innocence that children followed him as they might the Pied Piper. In place of the flute, Bill played a harmonica. He played with more heart than talent and with no more than a repertoire of three songs. Yet no one ever seemed to tire of listening to him play. He would tap his foot and his eyes would gleam with fire, as he made a music that enticed listeners to dance or tap their feet and clap along with him.

Bill's personal magnetism extended beyond children and adults. Animals also sensed something safe and appealing about him. He spoke to his creature friends with the same rapt attention he extended to his human friends. To Bill, all God's creatures were equal and deserving of respect.

I suspect it was these personal attributes that made Bill so suitable for the role of Santa Claus. It was Bill's fitness to play Santa more than anything else that attracted considerable attention and led to such invitations as the one Bill, with me as his escort, was about to fulfill.

In most respects, Bill was the perfect Santa Claus, except perhaps for the fact that he was Jewish. By this time, he was in his late sixties—the right age to play December's mythical hero. His short, roly-poly body could not have been better crafted for the part. Also, his beard was long, unruly, and touched with the right shade of gray. He loved to laugh. He had eyes that twinkled; he had feet that could not stop dancing (or prancing); and he had a spontaneous ho-ho-ho that made up about five percent of his entire vocabulary.

While so many wonderful opportunities were extended to Bill following the debut of the movie, there is one that stands out among the others. This was an invitation from social work students for Bill to come to Luther College in Decorah, Iowa. His visit was scheduled for December 7, 1982, about a week before the college's Christmas break. It was, unfortunately, also about six months prior to Bill's untimely death and about a year before the release of the sequel movie, *Bill on His Own*, which Barry had written.

Bill on His Own was a movie Barry thought needed to be made in order to correct some false impressions he believed had been made in the first movie. The unexpected success of the first movie had whetted the appetites of both Mickey Rooney and the Hollywood producer to gamble on a sequel. Rarely is a made-for-television movie followed by a sequel. When a film such as *Bill* strikes a special chord with the viewers, it more typically leads to a pilot of a television series based on the theme or central characters in the movie.

The invitation to visit Luther College came nearly a year after the airing of the first movie on Bill's life and, as noted, a year prior to the airing of the sequel, *Bill on His Own*. Students in the college's social work program had arranged for a daylong program that involved visits to local agencies serving persons with disabilities; a fancy, black-tie dinner honoring Bill, sponsored by the college president; and a showing of the first movie about Bill's life.

Owing to his limitations, Bill would require the assistance of a volunteer on such occasions. Usually the volunteers were drawn from the university's School of Social Work faculty. Most often, John Craft or I would get the assignment. On the occasion of the Luther College visit, it was my turn.

I knew I would have to pick up Bill very early on December 7 to get to Decorah, Iowa, in time to fulfill the expectations of our hosts. It was about 6:30 in the morning and still dark when I pulled up in front of Bill's boardinghouse in my rusty Toyota pickup truck. The streetlight cast just enough light to illuminate Bill standing at curbside, waiting for his ride. It was apparent he had been waiting for some time, even though I arrived exactly when I told Bill I would. Since Bill could not tell time, he had probably been awake half the night out of fear of missing his ride.

Without complaint, Bill piled into my car, his innocent face showing a shy grin. An early morning sleet had laced his magnificent gray beard with what looked like corn rows of slender icicles. It took nearly an hour to thaw him with my heater at full blast.

We drove in silence a good part of the way. The journey of less than 150 miles took nearly four hours due to the icy conditions of the highway. I drove slowly and methodically. The tension of the drive could not be avoided. My knuckles had turned white from the intensity with which I held the steering wheel. Bill, the unlikely celebrity, on the other hand, was totally at peace, dreaming only of the anticipated delights of yet another adventure.

It was Bill who broke the silence about a half hour into the ride. He said, "You know, buddy, I am really gonna joy this day, and we are gonna end it with a cold beer. You will buys me a beer if I do goods won't you, Tom?" I had little choice but to reply, "Of course, Bill."

In Decorah, the visits to the group homes, day centers, and sheltered workshops went splendidly. Bill, as the center of attention, grew more and more animated throughout the day. For a man nearing his seventh decade, he showed little sign of fatigue at shaking hands and handling the questions of his well-wishers.

It was obvious that Bill was a true folk hero to many of the special-population persons he met that day. Nearly everyone wanted his or her picture taken with Bill, plus his autograph. Fortunately, Bill had learned to scratch out a semilegible facsimile of his first name. He would write it BLL with the middle L dotted so that it could stand in for the I as well. For his fans, Bill would laboriously autograph the business cards I had had made for him and hand those out. The cards read, "William 'Bill' Sackter, Clinical Optimist and Proprietor Extraordinaire of Wild Bill's Coffeeshop."

By late afternoon, Bill and I were being escorted to the Luther College president's dinner party, which had been arranged in Bill's honor. The affair was held in one of those irreplaceable, century-old buildings emblazoned in Norwegian ethnic decor. Both town-and-gown dignitaries made up the forty or so guests at the dinner. Bill was seated at the head table, sandwiched between the college president and his wife. Unfortunately, I was seated far enough away that I would not be able to coach Bill on either meanings or manners.

I had had the foresight, however, to warn the planning committee about Bill's aversions to presidents, all of whom he associated with Richard Nixon. For whatever reason, Richard Nixon was known to Bill as a "donkey's ass." For those who knew Bill, Nixon was just about the only person whom he did not like. He did not even pretend to like him. Thus, the committee took great care to have all references to "college president" replaced by the academic title of "doctor."

The supper went flawlessly. Bill ravished both his meal and the voluminous attention he received. All who were seated near him seemed to enjoy his cheerful company thoroughly. After the meal, the president of Luther College gave a glowing testimonial about Bill, his generosity of spirit, and zest for living.

Bill was then invited to share a few words. Confidently, he rose from his seat, pranced to the podium, and with a well-fed grin said, "Thank yous very much for 'vitin' me. God's been good to me. I had some hard times, but now I gots the good times. I jus wish ever'buddy could be lucky as me. Thank you very much. God bless you. Shalom." Reflexively, Bill then reached into his pocket, pulled out his Hohner, and played his theme piece—the "Too Fat Polka."

The sincerity of Bill's offerings brought the dinner crowd to its feet. Their applause came from the heart. Bill could not have been happier, knowing he had pleased his supper companions. His eyes sparkled with enthusiasm, and a self-assured glow covered his face. This was Bill at his best.

It was in this spirit that Bill trotted off to the final event of the evening, the showing of his movie. The large college auditorium was filled with people of all ages. The townspeople who had come to see Bill actually outnumbered the college crowd.

To give Bill more of a role in this engagement, I had arranged for him to appear in a Santa suit on stage once the movie ended. He would wish the merriest of Christmases to all who attended. This finale had a nice tie-in with a visual postscript in the movie, which showed the real Bill dressed in a Santa outfit.

Bill could not have looked more the part than he did that night. As the movie drew to a close (his cue), Bill pranced to center stage in full dress. With a near perfect voice, he sang out the ho-ho-hos and Merry Christmases to his audience and shook a string of sleigh bells with the deftness of a professional percussionist. He ended, as he always did, with his "Thank you very much" speech and a harmonica tune. The audience loved him, and they had loved the movie.

Words cannot not capture the feeling in the air that night. A light snow had fallen and blanketed Decorah with a fresh coat of whiteness. The scenery, coupled with the stillness of this midweek evening, made the town resemble a Christmas-card version of Bethlehem. The full house that had come to see Bill and hear his story exuded the mellowness of a congregation at a midnight service on Christmas Eve.

The movie had held the audience spellbound. Bill's follow-up only added to the magic of the evening. No one seemed anxious to leave. Only when Bill climbed down from the stage did the audience snap out of its suspended state, as many a person rose to greet him.

Magic evening or not, I, as escort, was exhausted. I prodded Bill to hurry up and finish. I reminded him we had a similar appearance scheduled the following afternoon at Clark College in Dubuque. Naturally, Bill was not pleased by my attempt to rush, and in his way, he let me know it. He still had people to greet and personal cards to hand out.

When I finally weaned Bill away from his well-wishers, he reminded me of my promise to buy him a beer. After all, hadn't things gone well?

Unquestionably, it had been a spectacular day and evening. There would be no possible way to renege on my earlier promise. So I quickly gathered Bill's things and nudged him in the direction of the car.

We headed toward downtown, assuming it would be the most likely place to find an open tavern or bar. Unfortunately, a Norwegian Lutheran college town, just before finals week, is not going to be one of your big party towns. Locating a suitable bar or tavern ended up being a bit like locating a Gideon Bible in the Vatican.

Finally, after nearly a quarter of an hour, I spotted a seedy-looking tavern that still seemed to be doing business at the eleven o'clock hour. The tavern must remain nameless, as whatever marquee it may have carried was no longer present (if it had ever had one).

We somewhat uneasily entered the tavern and seated ourselves on the empty stools at the horseshoe-shaped bar. Another ten or so dedicated drinkers were sprinkled about the room in booths or at tables.

Bill and I were both showing signs of fatigue, I more so than Bill. The bartender, a tall, gangly man about Bill's age, who looked like he had not slept in days, approached us. The rest of the customers, who clearly fit the namelessness of the establishment, shifted their gaze in our direction.

I ordered a couple of drafts from the uninspired bartender. We sipped our drinks in silence. A few minutes into our refreshments, I got the feeling we were still being stared at. As unobtrusively as possible, I scanned the crowd and discovered their eyes were focused on Bill. I turned to see what they found so intriguing. When I looked at Bill through their eyes, what they were staring at was obvious. Bill was still dressed as Santa Claus.

He appeared oblivious to any stares, or perhaps if he did sense them, he felt them appropriate to his new station in life. As I looked at Bill, I could not help but wonder if he had not perhaps overly identified with his new role. After all, in my experience as a mental health social worker many a crack-minded fellow has thought of himself as a Jesus, Napoleon, or a J. Edgar Hoover. Why not a Santa Claus?

When we finally finished our drinks—I had refused Bill's request for a quick refill—we slipped off the stools and headed to the door. Until then, no one, not even the bedraggled bartender, had spoken so much as word. Yet as we were to pass through the door and into the wintry night, some slurred voices in soft unison whispered, "Good nighth, Santa." Bill reflexively whirled in their direction and, in a deep voice, said, "Ho, ho, ho, Merry Christmas, good buddies."

By the time this Christmas season ended, Bill had managed to live out his Santa identity another sixteen times. His reputation as the perfect Santa had spread throughout the Iowa City community. From child care centers to nursing homes, Bill was in demand. He even played Santa in the University of Iowa's annual glittery Christmas season event, "Cocoa and Carols." Bill was once again back on the Hancher Auditorium stage, where a year earlier the movie based on his life had premiered.

Bill loved to walk the streets of Iowa City in December in his Santa suit, a suit my mother had made for him several years earlier. The hundreds of Christmas greetings Bill received as Santa must have only reinforced his assumed identity. At least for the month of December, Bill was able to set aside any self-image of crack-mindedness.

To my mind, the man who would be Santa—was.

That December was the capstone of Bill's celebrity life, though he continued to travel and fulfill invitations right up until his death. His last gig, again in my company, was to a senior center in Ames, Iowa. It took place only a week before death would visit him in his sleep. Bill showed no less energy or enthusiasm on that occasion than he had at any other time in the celebrity phase of his life.

12

In the Shadow of an Oak Tree

The celebrity period of Bill's life was limited to two short years. Bill packed an immense amount into those years. Still, it was a shame that he could not have had more time to cherish the love and attention he was receiving. But for Bill, as for all living creatures, life is finite. In Bill's case, the end came sometime during the early morning hours of June 16, 1983.

It was Bill's landlady, Mae Driscoll, who found him dead in his recliner, after he failed to make his morning stop for breakfast. She found him fully dressed, with his lunch box by his side, as if ready to head for work. Bill always showered in the evening, dressed for work, then slept in his chair, so as to not miss his bus. Such was the price he paid for not being able to tell time.

Mae called the rabbi immediately to come to the 1311 Yewell Street boardinghouse to verify the death. The rabbi took responsibility for sending notice to Bill's friends and for making arrangements for Bill's funeral. As his guardian at the time, the rabbi was the only legal family of Bill's that could act on his behalf.

The first calls the rabbi made were to Barry and me. I was then working in the College of Medicine, and Barry had long since gone to Hollywood. I took it upon myself to notify the students and the faculty in the School of Social Work. I wrote the following note and distributed it to those associated with the school:

This morning God paid our friend Bill Sackter a call.
He said the time had come for Bill to join him. While Bill
would have liked to come to work, he knew this was a
calling that could not be refused. He regrets not being
able to serve you today, but knows you'll manage without
him. He thanks you for your many kindnesses over the
years and for giving him such "good times" after so many
years of "hard times."

P.S. Bill died peacefully and painlessly in his sleep this
morning of a blood clot in his leg.

As word of Bill's death reached the city and university, somewhere
someone made the decision to fly both the city and university flags at half-
mast. During my years in Iowa City, I had never before known the flags to be
flown at half-mast, although I am sure the deaths of presidents or university
dignitaries had occasioned such actions in the past.

One could sense a shadow had been cast over the community. One of
the community's rarest, most precious resources had been taken away. It did
not take much imagination to know how those on the early morning bus
must have felt when their man of many smiles and greetings was not waiting
at the bus stop for his ride that day. Word of Bill's death had spread so
quickly that the bus driver knew of the event within minutes of the rabbi's
response to Mae's call.

At the School of Social Work, the halls were silent except for the shock
talk that comes from those who are unprepared for the message. The need to
speak about Bill in soft tones was evident as clusters of faculty and students
shared bits of information about his death, followed by reminiscences about
his life. By midday, the initial shock seemed to have passed, and a new kind
of emotion blanketed the environment. The sadness of the morning hours
gave way to a more positive, upbeat recollection of the man who brought so
much peace and love to our midst.

John Craft, a man who had cared so deeply for Bill, seemed to set the
tone. He felt that Bill, in neither life nor death, would want to occasion
overwhelming sorrow or sympathy. Nor should we be overly sad at this
time. John witnessed that, for Bill, any event was a cause for celebration. As
the afternoon wore on, the wonderful stories we all knew and associated

with Bill were told and retold. Some new and delightful tales previously unknown were shared in the many discourses that took place.

Independently, many other friends and admirers were busy working out their own independent responses. One of the faculty, Craig Mosher, who was also a professional woodworker, insisted that Bill ought to be buried in a handcrafted, oak coffin. To him, Bill was a man of oak, who had provided a solid sturdy shelter under which many of us rested from time to time. Bill's side interests as a woodworker only confirmed his right to a fine oak casket. Mosher set out in search of someone who could build an oak casket on short notice. He managed to find such a craftsman in a neighboring town. And the job was completed in time.

Meanwhile, in the home of Professors Kristi Nelson and Paul Adams, their young daughter Sarah had chosen to do some large drawings, which she hoped to tape to Bill's casket during the funeral ceremony. They were expressions of her fondest wishes for Bill. These would be folded gently and placed within his coffin when the time came for it to be closed permanently.

Farther away, the Arizona Association of Retarded Citizens had informed the Arizona Legislature of Bill's death. At the governor's behest, an official group of three Arizonans were dispatched to the funeral. They were to carry the Arizona flag, which, like Sarah's drawings, would be draped over Bill's coffin and then be buried with him. Bill may not have been a native son of Arizona, but he had managed to become an endeared adopted son of the state.

In Minneapolis, J. D., who had become a regional Ronald McDonald, was packing his bags to attend the funeral. Riding with him would be the architect Steve Buetow and other friends who had been members of the Barry Morrow Blue Sky Band in the sixties. Barry, Bev, and the children, of course, were busily getting their suitcases ready to fly from California to Iowa City. The rest of the Morrows would be there as well, driving in from the Twin Cities.

The rabbi, naturally, was hastily making plans for the funeral at the Agudas Achim Synagogue. Somehow the nation's media had been notified, and many reporters headed to Iowa City to report on the funeral. Mickey Rooney, who had also been notified, made the decision to send a representative on his behalf. Mickey's wife and son would both attend the funeral and remain for various gatherings of well-wishers after the ceremony.

Although Bill had essentially lost all contact with any blood relatives, a few months earlier, Barry had managed to locate a cousin, Shirley, who lived in New York. Ironically, Shirley had made plans to visit Bill the summer of his death but had been cheated by a few short weeks. Nonetheless, she did attend the funeral and shared some interesting background notes to Bill's childhood about which we still knew so little.

The funeral was scheduled for and held on June 18 at 10:00 A.M. A group of six men were asked to serve as pallbearers. Included among them were Barry and John, Bill's former conservators; me, his former employer and woodworking companion; Craig Mosher, the other social work professor with woodworking interests; and two other men from the churches with which Bill was associated.

The yard in front of the synagogue gave the appearance of a movie set, owing to the number of television groups that had chosen to film the event. No TV crews were allowed inside the synagogue, so they had stationed themselves outside. Mixed among the estimated crowd of 350 persons were another ten or so local, state, and national reporters from the print media. The death of Bill Sackter had made national news and was reported on several network channels.

One could only ask over and over, why? Why should this simple, illiterate, crack-minded old man have captured the heart of America to the extent that he had? Bill must have touched something in the American soul that was hungry for expression. Those of us who knew him knew the answer to this question but would be hard-pressed to put these feelings into words. Yet in some ways, those feelings compose the essence of this book.

During the funeral, I sensed Bill was still with us. I imagined how he would have reacted to the funeral service and what he might have said:

Hey, buddy, this was one fine funeral. I've been to many of 'em, and this one was real downtown. My coffin was beautiful. Wished I could-a helped sand it down and goolash it. Me and Tom would have made it look even more special. Wished I could thank Sarah Adams for drawin' those nice pitchures. I got so many pitchures from childern round the world that I have several scrapbooks full of 'em. I hope John and Tom takes care of 'em for me and shares 'em with other peoples. It was real nice that the frens from Arizona could come. I lived in Minnesota, I likes Iowa, and now I got Arizona, too. Can't have too many places like that when you are free man, a citizen who can vote and all.

The rabbi, he sure knows how to do funerals. He seemed a little nervous, but I think he's not real comfortable round lotsa people. Not like Barrymor. My ol buddy Barrymor, he's like me. Likes to talks in front of peoples. He tol some real nice stories bout me at the funerals, but he likes to exaggerate a little. Even if his stories ain't always true, they makes for interestin' listenin'.

Could'n imagine all those peoples comin'. Lotsa frens. If I could count, I would-a counted 'em. Seems like I had lotsa frens after I got out of isstitution. God was good to me, gave me the good times. Some peoples say I was seventy years old when I dies, but I always thought I was thirty-four. Truffully, numbers muzzled my mind. Never could keeps them straight.

I wanna thanks my frens, specially Rabbi Portmans, for puttin' on a good funerals for me. Now I won't be able to run ol Wild Bill's Coffeeshop no more, so I hope Tom finds someone else to make coffees. Peoples in North Hall likes the coffee, and they like comin' to sit and talk. Maybe someones would be willin' to fill in for me since I got other things God wants me to do now.

I wanna say good-byes to all my frens, specially Mae, Kenny, and Angela. We made a pretty good familys. Say good-byes to Clay and Zoe, who I will miss more'n anythin'. Old John, Craig, Eleanor, Bev Sweets, and others at the school, take cares. Poor Tom, he'll jus have to find someone elses to help him with furnitures. I know God loves you all. I'm gonna prays for you peoples.

As the ceremony ended, the initial tension of the event was released. The mood of those present appeared to shift. Smiles graced the faces of most. Everyone seemed to know everyone else. Bill had brought together a local community with some peculiar networks that extended well beyond the little college town. People moved slowly. Soon a parade of cars headed out across the freeway (I-80, which ran east and west) to a small, shady pasture with a humble wood-framed sign that indicated this was the Jewish cemetery.

In the middle area, under a big oak, was a freshly dug grave site. The pallbearers slowly carried Bill to this final resting place. It appeared as if most of those who attended the synagogue service had followed on to the grave site. At least several hundred worked their way around the open grave, hoping at the same time to find a bit of shade. Others stood defiant of the hot midday June sun, transfixed by the ceremony. Beads of perspiration rolled down the faces of even those in the shade. There was enough breeze to move the leaves on the trees. It was as if the breeze were intended to help the leaves wave good-bye to a kindred spirit—the man of oak.

As the rabbi intoned the final words of the burial ceremony, an old engineer's hat, like Bill used to wear in the coffee shop, was thrown into the grave. It came to rest atop the Arizona flag, which still draped the foot end of the coffin. A child, who had picked some wildflowers in the cemetery, had tossed them into the grave. A bouquet of roses from an unknown source followed. Finally, the first shovelful of dirt was cast by the rabbi. Each of Bill's friends did likewise until the coffin was no longer visible from above.

There were only a few tears in the eyes of those who had followed Bill to his final destination, under the oak tree. Most faces were etched in reflective smiles; no doubt many were playing back some special moment in their lives they may have shared with Bill.

The women from the synagogue had prepared a lunch at the School of Social Work for those who wished to attend. While the media people were busy gathering their equipment and hurrying to make the evening news, many of Bill's friends returned to the repast and continued sharing their many stories and memories of a man who would not soon be forgotten.

A few days after the funeral, the rabbi, John, and I met in his tiny apartment to dispose of Bill's estate. Bill had been buried without a headstone since he had died a pauper. There had been barely money enough to pay for the coffin. The grave site was a gift of the synagogue.

Bill's possessions consisted of pictures of children and their drawings, many sent to him by mail. Others were gifts handed to him by second graders during the year he had visited their classes by special invitation.

There were albums of pictures taken during his many trips and numerous appearances in the several years prior to his death. He had boxes full of religious memorabilia, ranging from his yarmulke to statues of the Blessed Virgin and three-dimensional pictures of Christ, which lit up when plugged in. There were boxes of audiocassettes of religious music, polkas, and televangelists' sermons. There were hundreds of letters from well-wishers and troubled persons seeking Bill's intervention. Adults in prisons and children in residential treatment centers were the most common correspondents. Finally, there were clothes. Bill's largely unused wardrobe included dozens upon dozens of shirts, pants, and socks that had never been worn. Bill had always preferred a few favorite items, such as his bib overalls, which he would wear day in and day out. The rabbi explained that he kept buying Bill new clothes because he always had the impression that Bill had only a few things to wear.

There were some miscellaneous items: several harmonicas, old bags of birdseed, an unwrapped box of cigars, a well-used pipe and some stale Prince Albert pipe tobacco, a somewhat damaged set of false teeth, several pairs of unused glasses, a football sweatshirt with Bill's name and "Phoenix Wranglers" imprinted on it, the cowboy hat from Mickey Rooney, a carving knife, and a dozen very ugly wigs (with the exception of the one that Mr. Executive had made for our friend). This was an estate that called for no heirs. Bill's possessions were reboxed, labeled in his name, and placed in storage in the School of Social Work.

Following Bill's death, efforts were made by the State of Minnesota to lay claim on his estate. The state demanded payment of the costs of the institutional care he had received over the five final years he spent at Faribault State Hospital. Apparently, they had assumed that Bill had in some way profited from the films about his life and had some dollars hidden away in some bank. Needless to say, the rabbi was not pleased with this correspondence. He hastily called a news conference to announce his indignation at the manner in which this correspondence had come, especially since the same bureaucrats had made no effort to extend a note of sympathy about Bill's passing. This hit the national news hard and fast, and the Minnesota welfare bureaucrats immediately backed off and apologized, with the help of a little intervention by a Minnesota senator.

Some good did come from this unfortunate episode. The press write-up on the controversy caught the eye of a Waterloo gravestone dealer. The man and his wife wanted to donate a head marker for Bill's grave, and they did so as part of a separate ceremony conducted by the rabbi some months later.

Though years have passed since Bill died, hardly a day passes at the School of Social Work that memories of Bill don't surface in some capacity. At the time of this writing, for example, ABC television was in town to broadcast the Iowa and Penn State game for a national network audience. A call came to Wild Bill's Coffeeshop from ABC that the network would like to do a piece on the coffee shop for its halftime show.

Bill may be gone, but his legacy lives on.

13

Bill's Legacy

Bill used to like to say, "You can't have hair and brains both." Well, frankly, he had neither, which says something about their relative importance in life. What Bill did have, however, and in abundance, was heart and spirit. To that, one could easily add generosity, innocence, goodwill, gentleness, respect, and acceptance for others, plus a belief in God and the love of life.

It would be easy to confuse Bill's gifts as some sort of artifact of his mental retardation. Should we credit his simplicity, innocence, and goodwill to his being dumb? There are certainly a number of dumb people in the world and rarely are people attracted to them. But people were attracted to Bill. All kinds of people.

Look at Bill's list of buddies. First, there was Barry Morrow, the successful screenwriter turned producer. He loved Bill and brought him into the bosom of his family. Bill had something Barry wanted and needed. My belief is that Bill helped Barry understand the humanity factor, not as a part of a story to be told, but as essential to relationships.

Rabbi Portman found Bill uplifting for his own spiritual life and journey. His journey with Bill alongside was, for him, a metaphor for Judaism as a belief system. And Professor John Craft discovered that Bill had a philosophy of life that, to him, finally made sense. Bill taught him that life was a series of wonderful and delightful relationships to be experienced and that life provided the opportunity for the gift of giving through these relationships. Mae Driscoll viewed Bill as the quintessential man who could be saved—which gave her fundamentalist religious orientation a purpose.

As for myself, I felt I had found a rare specimen, a man without evil, a man of innocence, a man of love. It mattered not that Bill wasn't too bright, because I knew it was not his mental limits that produced his gentle, nonviolent ways. I believed that God had given the world a good man and that I had the good fortune to be able to share his company. My time with Bill, I am convinced, made me a better man—spiritual health by association so to speak.

In the Jewish tradition, there is a belief that every hundred years, God chooses thirty-six persons for a kind of sainthood (the Mother Teresa's Sisters of Charity types). These are those rare people who emanate a profound goodness that is expressed in their actions of everyday living. In Hebrew, the tradition is called Tzapikim and serves the purpose of alerting Jews to the fact that every person one may meet, however simple and unsuspecting, could be one of the thirty-six. Debra Pava, a friend of Bill's and former Hebrew education teacher, was convinced that Bill was one of the chosen.

I knew Bill on a daily basis for eight years, and while he did not work any miracles (except perhaps for enhancing Zoe's recovery from spinal meningitis), I would be hard-pressed not to agree with Pava's observation. The world has its share of good people, but Bill was special even in that category. Even the good people I have known in my lifetime have had some flaw, some noticeable dark spot in their personalities. Most have some history or moment of having fallen. I searched for this in Bill and did everything I could think of to provoke it. There were even moments when I would truly try to exploit his dumbness to uncover some hidden infestation of meanness or evil within him. I found none.

I often wonder about the many other friendships and associations Bill had that were outside of my view and knowledge. What was it that attracted people to Bill? The day-care moms, I suspect, saw the opportunity for Bill to become a surrogate grandparent for their children, perhaps even a safe man in the house for themselves. The students, separated from home and family, found an equally safe friend and companion in Bill. He was the sort of friend and companion who presented neither a sexual threat nor an intellectual threat, yet he could offer satisfying company when this was in short supply. Why go to the movie alone when you could invite Bill to go along? Why be unsure of yourself at a party, when in Bill's company you wouldn't have to perform, since all eyes would be on him?

Bill somehow always knew his role in these situations. He acutely intuited the needs of others and selflessly responded to fill them. He could be grandfather one moment, life of the party the next moment; a dutiful furniture refinisher one day, a hawker of balloons to children the next. He could be a Pied Piper leading a band of little children with his harmonica or a saintly old Jewish elder filling the synagogue with the seriousness of prayer. He could be a dutiful tenant to a needy landlady, or he could play a spritely elf, entertaining a busload of commuters on their way to work or school. Yet Bill was not merely a man of a thousand faces, but a man of a thousand hearts—which he shared with others, each according to his or her needs.

It is truly hard to imagine a person with so much love and generosity surviving the snake-pit culture to which he had been so viciously exposed for nearly a half-century. In the institution, Bill and other patients suffered brutal treatment and chronic deprecation of character. These actions were, fortunately, offset by a few acts of kindness from caring staff members. Yet the weight of the evidence shows the brutality outweighed the kindnesses. Why didn't the violence burrow deep into his character? Was his character already set by the time he arrived at Faribault as a seven-year-old inmate? Did his dumbness protect him from the evil around him? See no evil, hear no evil, do no evil? Did his religious nature nurture some power of inner being stronger than the forces outside of him?

We do know there was something already at work in Bill during his years of confinement. His tenderness and caregiving to the physically and mentally challenged inmates with whom he lived is well-documented and self-reported. Harold was only one of many distressed children, severely and profoundly retarded, that fell under his care. He fed them with the patience of a Job, washed and bathed them like a mother who had graduated first in prenatal class, and loved them like the children of God that he felt them to be. Perhaps it was from these repeated acts of caregiving that inner goodness is germinated. For Bill, having such a wonderful environment of friends and family in later life certainly contributed to the spiritual dimension of the man I find so hard to capture in words.

My own life experiences have brought me into contact with the likes of civil rights leader Father Groppi, social reformer Dorothy Day, and Mother Teresa, whose assignments have always been to serve the poorest of the poor. Imagine picking up dying people from the dirty streets of Calcutta, where lice and other vermin and deadly infections are commonplace. Yet Mother Teresa did collect these people, with her only goal being to nurse them into death with dignity. Father Groppi, Dorothy Day, and Mother Teresa all seemed to perform such acts with that same serenity that Bill exuded day in and day out. The acts of caregiving must nourish the soul in ways most of us will never know—because we fear such experiences or believe they will take away too much from our own pursuits.

Bill spoke of the fact that he had had a hard life in the institution, yet it had not made him hard. If anything, once in the right setting, he engaged in a love of life that never seemed to burn out. His joy in living was truly infectious, probably because it always involved the pursuit of wanting to make others happy. In moments when he could have had respite, he prowled the corridors of the school or walked the streets, sensing unhappiness and, in his innocent way, struggling to free victims from its clutches.

There is a story, however, that will better explain what I have just tried to say. Somewhere about midpoint in Bill's life in Iowa City, both Barry and I had left the School of Social Work to go to work for the Department of Family Practice in the College of Medicine. It was not long before I was asked to do some professional-courtesy counseling with members of the medical community. I had been asked to provide some marriage counseling for a couple, both of whom were medical residents. Unfortunately, their marriage had been pretty damaged by the time I was asked to see them. I had only seen them once or twice before one of them attempted suicide by taking an overdose of a prescription drug.

Thankfully, the resident survived, but some extended hospitalization followed. I wanted to visit this person as soon as possible, yet hesitated out of discomfort and guilt that I had somehow failed. Out of cowardice, I asked Bill if he would accompany me on my first visit. He was delighted. I did not explain the nature of the problem for which the resident had been hospitalized, although this became immediately known during the early moments of our visit.

It is hard to re-create exactly what happened in the ensuing exchanges between, Bill, myself, and my client. It is sufficient to say my client's despair and embarrassment over the attempted suicide almost disappeared entirely. Bill's antics distracted the client so much that I could literally feel the person's mood change. After Bill played his harmonica, he asked the resident if he could visit every day. He wanted to know if he could bring my client a peanut butter and jelly sandwich on his next visit.

On the following visit, Bill brought his tape recorder and a box of polka music cassettes, which he left with my client, much to the person's amusement. In the days that followed my client's discharge, the client made several visits to Bill's coffee shop and openly credited Bill with having contributed to the recovery process.

More puzzling to me was the spiritual side of Bill. He loved going to religious services. He relished the ritual of the ceremony and looked forward to attending a service as if it were a trip to an amusement park. He particularly thrived on Catholic services with the incense, brightly colored vestments, and colorful statues. Sitting next to Bill at Sunday mass was itself a spiritual experience. He would keep his head bowed and gradually become transfixed by his environment. He would mumble word sounds to participate in lay responses and would sing loudly without knowing the meaning of the words he was trying to mimic. His "Our Father" went something like this:

Are Father, art in heaben,
hollow be thy knee,
thigh kingdom come,
thigh will be done,
in dirt as it is in heaben.

Words did not matter much to Bill. He communicated at a different level. Sounds, voice inflections, and nonverbals were his avenues for sharing feelings and ideas.

Bill's spirituality, however, had little to do with the practice of religion. His spirituality was manifested in the way in which he saw reality and could reframe reality for himself and others. Life, according to Bill, was essentially good and beautiful. "I've a good life now, buddy" was a standard expression. He could not imagine life as otherwise since he felt God was good and God was everywhere. While his instincts helped him distance occasional human predators, his normal response to people was to believe in their goodness. In many ways, he had reason to. For the most part, he was enveloped in the world of some very exceptional people: Barry, the rabbi, Mae Driscoll, and Debbie Pava.

I am still haunted by Barry's story of Bill's trip to the hospital to visit his daughter, Zoe, who was gravely ill. Zoe had been in coma for several days as a result of having been stricken with spinal meningitis. Bill had been restricted from visiting because he was not a blood relative to the child. When the decision was finally made to allow Bill to visit, he entered the room, fell immediately into prayer, and moments later, Zoe came out of her coma. Why? Coincidence? Morphogenic resonance? Divine intervention?

There will be no real answer to the theories behind this event. Yet it does no harm to say that Bill's spirituality contributed to her recovery. I suspect Bill's spirituality contributed to his own health as well.

During his eight years at the School of Social Work, Bill never missed a workday, except for several days when he was hospitalized for his ulcerated leg. Faculty and students would struggle through the long Iowa winters with colds and flus, sometimes even a broken bone or two from a slip on the ice. Meanwhile, Bill would report to work without so much as a sniffle. He'd lumber in to work looking every bit the clumsy and fragile old man. Yet to watch him work or play, one could not help but admire his underlying athleticism and health.

Another of Bill's attributes deserving of comment was his nonviolent nature. Something attracted him to those who were angry or anguished. He searched them out for the purpose of siphoning off the venom that was eating away their capacity for goodwill. Bill had his methods. Conversations, compliments, and an occasional mesmerizing tune played on his harmonica were among his nonviolent tactics.

Moreover, Bill's generosity was notorious. A quarter in his pocket meant a candy bar for a child in the day care center. If someone asked him for a dollar, he was as likely to give the person five. Bill was particularly vulnerable to the television evangelists' requests on behalf of starving children in some part of the world. True, he could never distinguish the different values of paper money. Silver coins, on the other hand, he differentiated by size. To Bill, a nickel was always worth more than a dime. Nonetheless, he was generous to a fault with money, like the time he handed out quarters to everybody in the park during his visit to the nation's capital.

Food seemed to have greater value to Bill than money. He treasured his packed lunches and would proudly display their delectable contents to those around him. Still as hard as it was for Bill, if someone looked twice at one of his cookies, it was given. A person never had to ask, Bill just gave.

Perhaps his most generous quality was his total acceptance of those around him. He met no ugly people, no weird people, no evil people. He was the most nonjudgmental person I had ever met. To Bill, people were just people, and he wanted all of them to be his friends. Of those who got to know him, I knew of no one who became his nemesis. The closest was probably Kenny, his boardinghouse mate who, I suspect, experienced some jealousy of Bill, especially of Bill's sociability. Yet even Kenny, despite his agoraphobia, volunteered to serve as one of Bill's pallbearers.

All in all, there was good reason why Bill Sackter came to enjoy the public attention that he did. His was the story of one of the chosen ones so rarely found in our midst and even more rarely publicly identified. Bill, of course, would have been content being a simple man who made coffee, who served it in cups of kindness and shared with those within his reach. The public attention he received was our doing. It was meeting our needs, not his.

Those of us closest to him still stand behind our decision to have told Bill's story through the movie. The world needed the reminder of the real intent of the tradition of Tzapikim—that the least-suspected person among us may be God's gift to us. In this case, the gift came in the person of a man of limited intellect but with limitless heart.

Unlike Don Juan who left a trail of broken hearts, Bill had forged a trail of happy hearts. That trail is still visible and productive. His death was nonetheless untimely. His opportunity to impact others had opened up at a whole new level following the movie. Yet Bill lived only another two years after the first movie, magnificent years though they were. Fortunately, much of Bill's magic has not diminished, despite his life being cut short by a thrombosis. His legacy is far from being completed.

When Bill died, a decision had to be made about whether or not to continue operating the coffee shop. For a couple of weeks, it remained closed. Then one day, a woman by the name of Beverly McClelland showed up and wanted to speak with me. Bev was a plain-looking women in her early forties who functioned intellectually at about the same level as Bill. Her affect was pretty flat, and she definitely lacked Bill's outgoing charisma. She had met Bill on numerous occasions through their mutual involvement in an organization known as Independent Living. Independent Living was a support program to assist persons with mental deficiency to cope with their problems of everyday living.

Bev was outspoken in her interests. She wanted to replace Bill. She felt the School of Social Work should be obligated to keeping the coffee shop open, if only to honor Bill's name. Beyond that, she argued, there were lots of people in the Independent Living program who needed employment. She was one of them. Bev's self-advocacy was, in fact, the turning point in the school's decision to reopen the coffee shop.

As it turned out, the school's renewed commitment included increasing the scale of the operation and drawing more heavily upon the coffee shop to serve as a practicum site for its students. The school appointed an advisory committee for the coffee shop. A student manager was selected, and a faculty liaison person was appointed to provide administrative guidance to the student manager. The rest is history.

Incrementally, the coffee shop increased both its service and its staff. At one point, the project provided employment to thirteen physically and mentally challenged adults. Students and faculty continued to enjoy the coffee shop as a place for easy conversation and sociability. More nonuniversity persons were showing up as well.

Efforts were undertaken to improve the coffee shop's physical appearance. With the help of donors and volunteers, a new oak parquet floor was laid over the worn-out linoleum. Piece by piece, some beautiful round oak tables with solid wood chairs replaced the makeshift tables and chairs that had been used. The tables and chairs came from purchases at auctions or were obtained through university surplus. Some of Barry's photos of Bill were used to create a sort of gallery. A large photo of Bill, Barry, Mickey Rooney, and Dennis Quaid dominated the photo exhibit. A giant sympathy card prepared at the reception following the funeral hung nearby. On it were over a hundred signatures. A four-burner coffeemaker was added, along with a donated safe and a used refrigerator.

Business grew. Many vacationers from other parts of the United States would wander into the place because they had seen it on television or on video or had heard about it from friends. For years to come, a postcard or letter would arrive at the coffee shop from someone who was unaware of Bill's death. And the press somehow never grew tired of writing Bill's story or covering events associated with the coffee shop.

On the first anniversary of Bill's death, those involved with keeping the coffee shop running decided to organize a Bill Sackter Day. The main staple of this event was a dinner to which local persons with disabilities would be invited, along with students, faculty, and friends of Bill. It was a time for Bill's friends to get together and reminisce about Bill and the coffee shop. Since 1984, Bill Sackter Day has been a regular event, though the date on which it is celebrated has varied.

For two years following Bill's death, Bev McClelland was the lone worker in the coffee shop. Another worker, Ed Gaines, was hired part-time to handle the books. Neither Bill nor Bev were able to make change, let alone do any bookkeeping. Ed, on the other hand, though he suffered severely from cerebral palsy, had completed an Associate of Arts degree and had an accounting background.

Unfortunately, Bev had only been two years into the job when she succumbed to heart disease. Like Bill, she would be deeply missed, as she had grown to be a real friend to coffee shop regulars.

With a new start necessary, a decision was made by the advisory committee to add more staff and extend the hours of the coffee shop. A young man by the name of David, who like Bill had spent most of his life in a mental institution, was hired to replace Bev. David had been placed in a psychiatric facility at age seven and did not gain his release for twenty years. At this writing, both he and Ed Gaines have worked in the coffee shop steadily for more than a decade. David also began working for a spin-off project of Wild Bill's Coffeeshop—the refinishing of furniture and repair of collectibles and their resale through the coffee shop. Known as Junque City, it would become one of the best bargain shops for antique/collectible hunters in Iowa City.

Junque City has subsidized Wild Bill's Coffeeshop, whose expenses always manage to outrun its revenue. The coffee shop's deficit financing is both a product of reliance on student managers and the desire to overemploy staff because of the need and demand for semisheltered work opportunities in the area. Yet for all its ups and downs, financially and otherwise, the coffee shop has lasted for nearly a quarter century as a voluntary service.

A few years ago, the coffee shop and Junque City had enough surplus in savings to experiment with another venture—a second coffee shop like Bill's, to be located in the International Center. It was called Mr. Ed's, in recognition of its new proprietor, Ed Gaines. It had a two-year run and then closed. Operating the coffee shop demanded more physical strength and dexterity than Ed could provide, and student volunteers were not reliable enough to make up for his limitations. Like Bill's, Mr. Ed's had its moments of popularity and drew considerable local attention from the press.

After a few months operating Mr. Ed's, Ed became restless and began looking for something new to do. A grant was written on his behalf to the Iowa Department of Economic Development's small enterprise program. The proposal called for the development of a color supergraphics design service as a private, for-profit venture. The project was funded, and Mr. Ed's Supergraphics was duly incorporated and installed adjacent to Wild Bill's Coffeeshop. While Ed was not getting rich, he did report that he had never been happier in his life.

There have been a number of clones of Bill's Coffeeshop over the years, as students carried the concept into their social work practices elsewhere. The most famous of these is a restaurant that operates in downtown Rock Island, Illinois. This restaurant provides employment for some ninety persons who suffer from chronic mental illness, and it serves a downtown business clientele. The restaurant also doubles in the evening hours as a drop-in center for its workers and others who share their disabilities.

Over the past two decades, Wild Bill's Coffeeshop has been home to several AA groups; it has served as a setting for a marriage of one of the secretaries; it has been used by rhetoric instructors as a location to meet with students; it has served as a meeting place for groups as diverse as a gay-lesbian alliance and a Christian student association.

Nearly seven years ago, Bob Finch, a former social work student with multiple sclerosis, asked if he couldn't use the coffee shop on Friday nights to sponsor coffeehouses for local musicians. Bob, although quadriplegic, began serving as impresario for Bill's Coffeehouse. Bob had been a musician himself before his progressive disease no longer allowed him to play guitar. Finding and promoting local folk musical talent became a way of continuing his musical interests while being of service to other musicians. When Bill Sackter Day rolls around, it is Bob Finch and his local talent pool that provides much of the evening program.

At a recent Bill Sackter Day anniversary gathering, Barry Morrow returned to address those in attendance with his reflections on Bill's legacy. His talk was entitled "From Bill to Babbit." He spoke to the common denominator of his two most famous scripts, *Bill* and *Rain Man*.

In his talk, Barry pointed out how the movie *Bill* had opened up a new genre of film that presents persons with handicaps in a more positive and endearing light. Prior to the debut of the movie, most mentally challenged people were presented as ominous figures, often dangerous and grotesque. In a few cases, where the physically or mentally challenged received sympathetic treatment, such as *Phantom of the Opera* or *Elephant Man*, the films exploited their physical strangeness to create audience appeal.

However, in the post-Bill era, there have been wonderful films like *Rain Man, My Left Foot*, and *Forrest Gump*. *Rain Man* and *Forrest Gump* were extraordinary box-office hits. Interestingly, Barry Morrow was a writer in two of the four, and it was the film about Bill that started it all.

What was Bill's continuing impact on Barry? Without Bill's story, would Barry have enjoyed a Hollywood career with the same success? No one, of course, will ever know for sure. The fact remains, it was old Bill who gave Barry his lucky two-dollar bill when Barry was departing for California to pursue his career in film. Barry had the talent, but Bill was the catalyst.

Bill died over a decade ago. What legacy did he leave the other people who were so closely associated with him—the rabbi, Tom, John, Eleanor, Mae, Kenny, and dozens of unknown others? Of course, it is virtually impossible to measure the actual extent of any ongoing influences. The rabbi has continued his spiritual leadership at the synagogue. I returned to the School of Social Work from the College of Medicine and continue to serve as the permanent faculty liaison to the coffee shop. John Craft died with a smile on his face. Eleanor retired and leaves her gardening only to return for Bill Sackter Day events. John Anders is retired and lives near his daughter in California. Kenny got on his motorcycle and returned to Colorado and has not been heard from since. Angela is in a nursing home, still walking her doll—only now up and down corridors rather than around the block. Mae finally joined her maker and is probably cooking for old Bill once more. I am convinced they are in the same place.

It is apparent to me that Wild Bill's Coffeeshop still resonates with Bill's generous spirit and will do so until the university bureaucracy decides to replace it with vending machines. The coffee shop remains an anomaly in a corporate university, or perhaps more imaginatively stated, it is a social oasis in what is otherwise a desert. The university has never quite known what policy to follow with respect to the project. Bill's Coffeeshop has never contributed to its image as a leading scholarly institution, which is essentially the kind of publicity with which the university likes to associate itself. On the other hand, it has never openly rejected the human face it put on the university through the films and the many news articles. Imagine getting positive name recognition out to 200 million people internationally without having to invest a dime. Even today, Bill's Coffeeshop is self-supporting and to a slight extent profit-generating. Any surplus goes into projects that benefit either the university or the community.

The ambivalence of the university toward the whole phenomenon surrounding Bill came to a head after Bill's death. While the university flew its flag at half-mast, no official word of condolences was ever received from upper administration nor did any university person officially attend Bill's funeral. The effort to have North Hall renamed Sackter Hall in memory of Bill has been repeatedly ignored.

Nonetheless, the university has let the coffee shop project survive and has accepted its role as a service-learning site. It will be interesting to see what the future holds for Bill's Coffeeshop as the university continues to undergo essential changes.

Bill's legacy hopefully will be able to continue on its creative journey. Barry is committed to doing a documentary that will show the world even more of the real Bill than could be realized in the filmed, semifictional versions of his life.

The Arc has chosen to rename its national research and demonstration center the Bill Sackter Center for Self-Determination. The local Iowa City Summer Arts Festival in cooperation with Harmonicas over Iowa has inaugurated an annual Bill Sackter Harmonica Festival. And for my part, I hope my biographical sketches of Bill and his buddies will help to stimulate renewed interest in giving Bill a small place in American mythology.

Appendix: The Accomplishments of an Unlikely Celebrity, Bill Sackter

1977	Chosen Iowa's Handicapped Citizen of the Year by Governor's Committee on Employment of the Handicapped. Chosen for second place, United States Handicapped Citizen of the Year by U.S. Department of Health and Human Services, Division of Developmental Disabilities.
	Spent a weekend in Washington, D.C., as guest of Senator Dick Clark of Iowa.
1978	Received Presidential Award, Annual Meeting of the American Academy for Cerebral Palsy and Developmental Medicine.
	Began playing Santa Claus for local Iowa City organizations.
1979	Played Santa Claus for patients at Mercy Hospital, Iowa City.
	Celebrated Bar Mitzvah at age 66.
1980	Played Santa at his own event—Bill's Christmas party for Iowa City children at the downtown shopping mall.
1981	Visited Mickey Rooney on the movie set of *Bill* in Dallas, Texas. Later attended a performance of *Sugar Babies* and was brought on stage by Rooney, the show's star.

Attended the sold-out premiere of *Bill* at Hancher Auditorium, University of Iowa, Iowa City. (The movie was later shown on network television.)

1982   Accepted the Golden Globe Best Actor Award on behalf of Mickey Rooney for his performance in *Bill*, during a nationally televised event. (Rooney and cowriter Barry Morrow would later receive Emmy Awards for *Bill*.)

Played Santa Claus for University of Iowa holiday event, "Cocoa and Carols," at Hancher Auditorium, Iowa City.

Received special award, Rock Island Chapter of the Association of Retarded Citizens.

Received special recognition, Southeast Iowa Goodwill Industries.

Received news media award, presented by the Awareness Communication Team for the Developmentally Disabled, Detroit, Michigan.

Received certificate of recognition from Wilson Elder Service Center.

Given Beverly Enterprise Award for special service to nursing home residents, Beverly Manor, Iowa City.

Appeared as special guest of the Grand Marshall of Faribault (Minnesota) Days Celebration.

Received special recognition, National Association of Retarded Citizens meeting, Dallas, Texas.

Received special recognition, Cedar Rapids (Iowa) Executive Club.

Received special recognition, Iowa Association for Retarded Citizens, Waterloo, Iowa.

Given the Outstanding Contribution to Intergenerational Understanding Award (with Barry Morrow), Mid-America Congress on Aging, Kansas City, Missouri.

Appeared as special guest, Cedar Rapids (Iowa), Knights of Columbus.

Appeared as special guest and gave harmonica performance, Clinton Community College, Clinton, Iowa.

Appeared by special invitation, Dubuque (Iowa) Art Fair.

Received special award, Annual Convention of Illinois Association of Retarded Citizens, Chicago, Illinois.

Named in special proclamation by Governor Mario Cuomo, New York State Rehabilitation Program, Albany, New York.

Given special award, Arizona Association of Retarded Citizens, Phoenix, Arizona.

Given Honorary Citizen of the State recognition, Arizona State Legislature.

Appeared as halftime guest, Phoenix Wrangler professional football team.

1984   The American Association of Retarded Citizens (now known as the Arc) established a National Bill Sackter Award to be given at its annual meeting in Dallas, Texas.

Before his death on June 16, 1983, Bill was invited to several upcoming events. He was to have been an honored guest at the University of Iowa Homecoming in the fall and was to have participated in welcoming the parents of freshmen. He was also to have been declared an official ambassador for mentally retarded citizens by the White House. In December 1983, a second movie about his life, *Bill on His Own*, was shown on network television.

Thomas Walz teaches social work at the University of Iowa. He received his B.A. from Saint John's University (Minnesota), his M.A. from Saint Louis University, and his Ph.D. from the University of Minnesota. He has been an Oberman Fellow in Developmental Disabilities and a visiting professor in gerontology at the University of Hawaii and at Perm University in Russia. The founder and director of the annual National Creative Writing Seminar for Social Workers at the University of Iowa, he has published many short stories, poems, and editorials.